USA 1919–1941

GCSE Modern World History for Edexcel

USA 1919–1941

GCSE Modern World History for Edexcel

Steve Waugh
John Wright

HODDER
EDUCATION
AN HACHETTE UK COMPANY

This material has been endorsed by Edexcel and offers high-quality support for the delivery of Edexcel qualifications. Edexcel endorsement does not mean that this material is essential to achieve any Edexcel qualification, nor does it mean that this is the only suitable material available to support any Edexcel qualification. No endorsed material will be used verbatim in setting any Edexcel examination, and any resource lists produced by Edexcel shall include this and other appropriate texts. While this material has been through an Edexcel quality-assurance process, all responsibility for the content remains with the publisher. Copies of official specifications for all Edexcel qualifications may be found on the Edexcel website – www.edexcel.org.uk.

The Publishers would like to thank the following for permission to reproduce copyright material:

Photo credits
p. 8 © Hulton-Deutsch Collection/ CORBIS; **p. 9** Peter Newark American Pictures/ Bridgeman Art Library; **p. 10** Peter Newark American Pictures/ Bridgeman Art Library; **p. 12** © Ullsteinbild/ Topfoto; **p. 13** Mary Evans Picture Library; **p. 14** © Bettmann/ CORBIS; **p. 15** © Topham Picturepoint; **p. 16** *t* and *b* © Bettmann/ CORBIS; **p. 17** © Swim Ink 2, LLC/ CORBIS; **p. 18** © Ullsteinbild/ Topfoto; **p. 19** *l* © Bettmann/ CORBIS; **p. 19** *r* Library of Congress; **p. 20** *l* © CORBIS; **p. 20** *r* Granger Collection, New York/ Topfoto; **p. 22** © Bettmann/ CORBIS; **p. 23** © Bettmann/ CORBIS; **p. 24** Library of Congress; **p. 25** © Bettmann/ CORBIS; **p. 27** Peter Newark American Pictures/ Bridgeman Art Library; **p. 28** *l* and *r* Library of Congress; **p. 32** © Bettmann/ CORBIS; **p. 33** Granger Collection, New York/ Topfoto; **p. 35** *l* © Bettmann/ CORBIS; **p. 35** *r* © CORBIS; **p. 36** © Bettmann/ CORBIS; **p. 37** © Bettmann/ CORBIS; **p. 39** Granger Collection, New York/ Topfoto; **p. 40** © Bettmann/ CORBIS; **p. 41** Library of Congress; **p. 42** © Bettmann/ CORBIS; **p. 43** *l* © Bettmann/ CORBIS; **p. 43** *r* Library of Congress; **p. 45** Granger Collection, New York/ Topfoto; **p. 47** Ohio State University; **p. 48** *l* and *r* Library of Congress; **p. 50** *l* Peter Newark American Pictures/ Bridgeman Art Library; **p. 50** *r* Library of Congress; **p. 51** *l* Library of Congress; **p. 51** *r* Granger Collection, New York/ Topfoto; **p. 55** Library of Congress; **p. 56** Peter Newark American Pictures/ Bridgeman Art Library; **p. 58** © Bettmann/ CORBIS; **p. 59** © Bettmann/ CORBIS; **p. 60** © Bettmann/ CORBIS; **p. 62** Library of Congress; **p. 66** © Bettmann/ CORBIS; **p. 67** © Ullsteinbild/ Topfoto; **p. 70** © Ullsteinbild/ Topfoto; **p. 71** © Bettmann/ CORBIS; **p. 73** AP/Wide World Photos; **p. 76** © Bettmann/ CORBIS; **p. 78** Topfoto/AP; **p. 79** © Bettmann/ CORBIS; **p. 80** © Bettmann/ CORBIS; **p. 81** © Bettmann/ CORBIS; **p. 82** Library of Congress; **p. 87** Granger Collection, New York/ Topfoto; **p. 88** © Bettmann/ CORBIS; **p. 90** © Bettmann/ CORBIS; **p. 91** © Bettmann/ CORBIS; **p. 92** Library of Congress; **p. 94** *l* Granger Collection, New York/ Topfoto; **p. 94** *r* Library of Congress; **p. 96** Library of Congress; **p. 99** *l* Peter Newark American Pictures/ Bridgeman Art Library; **p. 99** *r* Photo courtesy FDR Library; **p. 102** © New York Daily News, L.P., reprinted with permission; **p. 103** Brown Brothers; **p. 104** Peter Newark American Pictures/ Bridgeman Art Library; **p. 105** Brown Brothers; **p. 107** © Bettmann/ CORBIS; **p. 111** *t* and *b* courtesy Tennessee Valley Authority; **p. 113** © CORBIS; **p. 114** © Bettmann/ CORBIS; **p. 115** *all* © Bettmann/ CORBIS; **p. 116** Punch Library and Archive; **p. 122** Photo courtesy FDR Library; **p. 123** © Bettmann/ CORBIS; **p. 124** Peter Newark American Pictures/ Bridgeman Art Library; **p. 125** Peter Newark American Pictures/ Bridgeman Art Library.

Acknowledgements
p. 7 Edexcel Limited; **p. 8, 34** *l*, **77** *ml*, **81** *tl* and **89** *r* T Triggs, *Boom and Slump in Inter-war America*, Nelson Thornes, 1987; **p. 9, 33, 39, 54** *ml*, **59** *mr*, **63** *tr* and **71** B Walsh, *Modern World History*, J. Murray, 2001; **p. 11** *tl*, **20, 43, 46** *mr*, **53** *tl*, **53** *ml*, **54** *bl*, **56, 59** *tl*, **64** *l*, **64** *r*, **73** *bl* and **112** *tl* R Mills, C White, M Samuelson, *The USA Between the Wars 1919–41*, Hodder Murray, 1998; **p. 11** *br*, **37** *br*, **123** *ml* and **123** *bl* T Lancaster and D Peaple, *The Modern World*, Causeway, 2000; **p. 14** *bl* Harriet Ward, *USA: From Wilson to Nixon, 1917–75*, Collins Educational, 1996; **p. 15** *br* M Chandler and J Wright, *Modern World History for Edexcel*, Heinemann Education, 2001; **p. 14** *mr*, **73** *tl*, **124** and **125** N Smith, *The USA 1917–1980*, Oxford University Press, 1996; **p. 14** *br* J Rublowsky, *After the Crash: America in the Great Depression*, Crowell-Collier Press, 1970; **p. 15** *l* P Sann, *The Lawless Decade*, Outlet, 1957; **p. 17, 69** *mr* and **69** *tr* C K Macdonald *Modern America*, Simon and Schuster Education, 1987; **p. 21** Reprinted on the website of the Miller Center of Public Affairs, University of Virginia, at http://millercenter.org/academic/americanpresident/hoover; **p. 30** John Vick, *Modern America*, Irwin, 1985; **p. 34** *l*, **36, 38, 57, 60, 65** and **69** *ml* P Mantin, *The USA, 1919–41*, Hodder, 2002; **p. 37** *tl* Reprinted on *The Jazz Age: Flapper Culture and Style* at www.geocities.com/flapper_culture/; **p. 37** *ml* and **41** D and S Willoughby *The USA, 1917–45*, Heinemann Education, 2000; **p. 37** *mr* S Waugh, *Essential Modern World History*, Nelson Thornes, 2001; **p. 42** Reprinted on Wikipedia at http://en.wikipedia.org/wiki/Hays_Code; **p. 49** D Kyvig, *Repealing National Prohibition*, University of Chicago Press, 1979; **p. 59** *tr* Reprinted on Spartacus Educational at www.spartacus.schoolnet.co.uk/USAsacco.htm; **p. 62** P Shuter, *Skills in History*, Heinemann, 1988; **p. 69** *mr* P Sauvain, *Key Themes of the Twentieth Century* Nelson Thornes, 1996; **p. 72** Carl Sandburg, *The People, Yes*, Harcourt, Brace, 1936; **p. 73** *ml* T Lancaster and D Peaple, *Toledo: A City the Auto Ran Over*, Survey Graphic, 1930; **p. 75** Adapted from a text reprinted on Spartacus Educational at www.spartacus.schoolnet.co.uk/USAwallstreet.htm; **p. 77** *tl* Reprinted on the website of The Herbert Hoover Presidential Library and Museum at http://hoover.archives.gov/exhibits/Hooverstory/gallery07/gallery07.html; **p. 77** *bl* Reprinted on "The Unofficial Doc and Merle Watson and semi-official Woody Guthrie and Almanac Singers Site at http://www.geocities.com/Nashville/3448/alliwant.html; **p. 80** *ml* J Simkin *Evidence and Empathy: America in the Twenties*, Spartacus, 1986; **p. 80** *bl* F L Allen *Since Yesterday: The Nineteen-thirties in America*, H. Hamilton, 1940; **p. 81** *ml* W J Bennett, *America: The Last Best Hope, Volume 2*, Nelso Current, 2007; **p. 82** *tr* Reprinted on Wikiquote at http://en.wikiquote.org/wiki/Herbert_Hoover; **p. 86** Robert S McElvaine, *The Depression and the New Deal: A History in Documents*, Oxford University Press, 2000; **p. 87** *r* and **92** *bl* Studs Terkel, *Hard Times: An Oral History of the Great Depression*, Pantheon Books, 1970; **p. 88** *tr* I Bernstein, *The Lean Years: A History of the American Worker, 1920–1933*; Houghton Mifflin, 1960; **p. 90** B Cabell Phillips, *From the Crash to the Blitz, 1929–1939*; Macmillan, 1969; **p. 91** *tr* Dorothea Lange, *The Assignment I'll Never Forget: Migrant Mother*, Popular Photography, 1960; **p. 91** *mr* J Steinbeck, *The Grapes of Wrath*, Viking, 1939; **p. 96** Daniel Bonevac, ed, *Today's Moral Issues: Classic and Contemporary Perspectives*, Mayfield, 1992; **p. 97** *tl* Reprinted on the website of the Mackinac Center for Public Policy at www.mackinac.org/article.aspx?ID=4026; **p. 97** *bl* Reprinted on Spartacus Educational at www.spartacus.schoolnet.co.uk/USAhoover.htm; **p. 97** *tr* R Smalley, *Depression and the New Deal* Longman, 1990; **p. 98** *l* A Hatch, *Franklin Roosevelt: An Informal Biography*, H. Holt, 1947; **p. 98** *r* and **102** *bl* F Perkins, *The Roosevelt I Knew*, Viking, 1946; **p. 100** *tl* Reprinted on History Matters at http://historymatters.gmu.edu/d/5057/; **p. 102** *ml* Reprinted on the website of The Franklin D. Roosevelt Presidential Library and Museum at www.fdrlibrary.marist.edu/031233.html; **p. 102** *mr* D Brogan, *The Era of Franklin D. Roosevelt: A Chronicle of the New Deal and Global War*, Yale University Press, 1950; **p. 103** 'The Intent of the CCC', 8th April 1933, © 1933 Newsweek, Inc. All rights reserved. Reprinted by permission; **p. 104** *mr* Reprinted on the website of the Mid-Hudson Regional Information Center at www.mhric.org/fdr/chat3.html; **p. 104** *br* B W Beacroft and M A Smale, *The Making of America*, Longman, 1972, © Pearson Education Limited; **p. 105** W Leuchtenburg, *Franklin. D. Roosevelt and the New Deal*, Harper and Row, 1963; **p. 106** J Huxley *TVA: Adventure in Planning* Architectural Press, 1943; **p. 108** *The New Deal in Review 1936–40*, © The New Republic, 1940; **p. 110** D B O'Callaghan, *Roosevelt and the United States*, Longman, 1966, © Pearson Education Limited; **p. 112** *tr* Reprinted at www.traditionalmusic.co.uk/bluegrass-songbook/003650.HTM; **p. 121** *tl* H Zinn, *New Deal Thought*, Bobbs-Merrill, 1966; **121** *ml* J Patterson, *America in the Twentieth Century*, Harcourt Brace Jovanovich, 1976.

Every effort has been made to trace all copyright holders, but if any have been inadvertently overlooked the Publishers will be pleased to make the necessary arrangements at the first opportunity.

Although every effort has been made to ensure that website addresses are correct at time of going to press, Hodder Education cannot be held responsible for the content of any website mentioned in this book. It is sometimes possible to find a relocated web page by typing in the address of the home page for a website in the URL window of your browser.

Orders: please contact Bookpoint Ltd, 130 Milton Park, Abingdon, Oxon OX14 4SB. Telephone: (44) 01235 827720. Fax: (44) 01235 400454. Lines are open 9.00 – 5.00, Monday to Saturday, with a 24-hour message answering service. Visit our website at www.hoddereducation.co.uk.

© John Wright, Steve Waugh 2005, 2009
First published in 2005
This second edition published 2009 by
Hodder Education
An Hachette UK company
338 Euston Road
London NW1 3BH

Edited and designed by White-Thomson Publishing/Steven Maddocks/www.wtpub.co.uk

Impression number   5 4 3 2 1
Year   2013 2012 2011 2010 2009

ISBN: 978 0340 984 413

Cover photos: Henry Guttmann/ Getty Images (left) and Bettmann/ CORBIS (right)

Printed in Italy

A catalogue record for this title is available from the British Library.

Essex County Council Libraries

Contents

Introduction

About the course

During this course you must study four units:

- **Unit 1** Peace and War: International Relations 1900–1991
- **Unit 2** Modern World Depth Study
- **Unit 3** Modern World Source Enquiry
- **Unit 4** Representations of History.

These units are assessed through three examination papers and one controlled assessment:

- In Unit 1 you have one hour and 15 minutes to answer questions on three different sections from International Relations 1900–1991.
- In Unit 2 you have one hour and 15 minutes to answer questions on a Modern World Depth Study.
- In Unit 3 you have one hour and 15 minutes to answer source questions on one Modern World Source Enquiry.
- In the controlled assessment you have to complete a task under controlled conditions in the classroom (Unit 4).

Modern World Depth Study (Unit 2)

There are three options in the Modern World Depth Study unit. You have to study one. The three options are:

- **Option 2a** Germany 1918–39
- **Option 2b** Russia 1917–39
- **Option 2c** The USA 1919–41.

About the book

This book covers the key developments in the USA from 1919 to 1941. The book is divided into four key topics, each with three chapters.

- **Key Topic 1** examines the US economy in the years 1919–29. In particular, it focuses on the reasons for the boom of the 1920s and its effects

on the USA; and the problems of declining industry and agriculture.
- **Key Topic 2** explores US society in the years 1919–29. It focuses on the 'roaring twenties'; Prohibition and gangsters; and racism and intolerance.
- **Key Topic 3** concentrates on the Depression of 1929–33, especially the causes and consequences of the Wall Street Crash; the reaction of the US government during this period; and the impact of the Depression on people's lives.
- **Key Topic 4** examines Roosevelt's policies, particularly the key features of the New Deal; reasons for opposition; and the extent of economic and social recovery in the years 1933–41.

Each chapter in this book:

- contains activities – some develop the historical skills you will need, others are exam-style questions that give you the opportunity to practise exam skills. The exam-style questions are highlighted in blue.
- gives step-by-step guidance, model answers and advice on how to answer particular question types in Unit 2.
- defines key terms and highlights glossary terms in bold the first time they appear in each key topic.

About Unit 2

Unit 2 is a test of:

- knowledge and understanding of the key developments in the USA in the years 1919–41
- the ability to answer brief and extended essay-type questions and a source inference question.

You have to answer the following types of questions. Each requires you to demonstrate different historical skills:

- **Source inference** – getting messages from a source
- **Causation** – explaining why something happened
- **Consequence** – explaining the effects or results of an event
- **Change** – explaining how and why changes occurred
- **Describe** – giving a detailed description, usually of the key events in a given period – this is also known as the key features question

- **Judgement** – assessing the importance of causes, changes or consequences. This is commonly known as the **scaffolding** question.

Below is a set of specimen questions (without the source). You will be given step-by-step guidance in Chapters 2–12 on how best to approach and answer these types of questions.

This is a **source inference** question. You have to get a message or messages from the source.

This is a **describe** question – you have to describe the key features of historical actions or events.

This is a **consequence** question – you have to explain the effects or results of an event.

This is a **causation** question – you have to explain why something happened.

This is a **change** question – you have to explain how and why changes occurred.

This is a **scaffolding** question, which gives you four main points. You should develop at least three clear points and judge and explain the importance of each.

EXAM

UNIT 2

1(a) What does Source A tell us about the impact of the First World War on the economy of the USA?

(4 marks)

1(b) Describe US government policies towards industry in the 1920s.

(6 marks)

1(c) Explain the effects that developments in the car industry had on the US economy in the 1920s.

(8 marks)

1(d) Explain why there was a depression in US agriculture in the 1920s.

(8 marks)

2 Explain how the role of women in US society changed in the 1920s.

(8 marks)

3 Was over-production the main reason for the Wall Street Crash of 1929? Explain your answer.

You may use the following information to help you with your answer:

- Over-production
- Unequal distribution of incomes
- Protection
- Problems in the stock market

(16 marks)

(Total 50 marks)

Key Topic 1: The US economy 1919–29

Source A: Dozens of automobiles travel down a road lined with cherry trees near the Jefferson Memorial, 1920s

Source B: From a speech by a Republican Party politican in 1928

A car in every garage and a chicken in every pot? No, TWO cars in every garage and TWO chickens in every pot.

Task

What do Sources A and B show you about the economy of the USA in the 1920s?

This key topic examines the major issues in the economy of the USA from the end of the First World War to the **Wall Street** Crash in 1929. This was a time of boom and bust for the USA. At the beginning of the 1920s, Americans thought that their country would prosper and that all its citizens might become wealthy. At the end of the period, however, the Wall Street Crash ushered in a period of **depression** during which more than sixteen million people were unemployed and the country faced economic ruin.

Each chapter explains a key issue and examines important lines of enquiry as outlined below:

Chapter 1 The causes and consequences of the ecomomic boom (pages 9–20)

- Why did the US economy experience an economic boom in the 1920s?
- How important was the car industry?
- Why was there a boom in the **stock market**?
- Which other industries experienced a boom?

Chapter 2 Declining industries (pages 21–26)

- Why did some industries fail to experience a boom in the 1920s?
- What happened to the workers in the so-called 'sick industries'?

Chapter 3 Problems in agriculture (pages 27–31)

- Why did agriculture experience a period of prosperity in the years to 1920?
- Why was there overproduction in agriculture in the USA?
- Why did many agricultural workers become unemployed in the 1920s?

The causes and consequences of the economic boom

Source A: *The Builder,* a painting (1920s) by the American artist Gerrit Beneker

Source B: A graph comparing US industrial production to that of the rest of the world

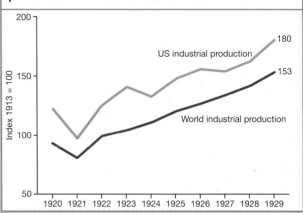

Tasks

1. *What is the message of the painting?*

2. *What can you learn from Source B about US industrial production in the 1920s?*

The American economy greatly benefited from the First World War, and in the 1920s the USA enjoyed an economic boom which was encouraged by the policies of successive Republican presidents as well as the advanced production techniques that the car industry began to use. There was a rapid growth in newer industries together with a dramatic rise in the values of **stocks and shares** on the US stock market.

This chapter answers the following questions:

• Why did the USA experience an economic boom in the 1920s?
• Why was there a boom in the stock market?
• How important was the car industry?
• Which other industries experienced a boom?

Examination skills
This chapter covers a range of question types that you will have to answer in Unit 2.

Why did the USA experience an economic boom in the 1920s?

A boom occurs when the economy of a country is rapidly developing. Factories make and sell a lot of goods. The money generated is put back into the factories, which then make and sell more goods and generate even more money. In other words, an economy experiences the multiplier effect, whereby the growth of one industry benefits and stimulates the growth of another. In the USA in the 1920s:

- The growth of the car industry benefited the rubber and glass industries.
- The development of electricity stimulated the growth of new industries which made electrical products such as vacuum cleaners and fridges.

The US boom can be attributed to a number of long-term factors, such as the availability of natural resources and a cheap labour force and the impact of the First World War. More immediate factors included the policies of the Republican governments, technological change, **consumerism**, the availability of **credit**, a general atmosphere of confidence and **isolationism**.

Natural resources

The USA had a plentiful supply of raw materials, including oil, coal, wood and iron. These resources had provided the foundation for US economic growth in the years before the First World War and stimulated further growth in the 1920s.

Cheap labour force

There was continuous immigration from Europe to the USA in the years before the First World War. This provided a plentiful supply of cheap, unskilled labour from Germany, Scandinavia, Italy, Poland, Russia, Ireland, China and Japan.

The impact of the First World War

The USA did not enter the First World War until 1917. Its economy benefited greatly from the war.

Source A: This cartoon (1880) shows the willingness of the USA to take in people who felt they had to leave their own country

Indeed, by 1918 the USA was the world's leading economy.

- The war was fought in Europe and badly affected the economies of leading European countries – notably Britain, France and Germany, which had to divert their resources to the war effort.
- These countries bought much-needed supplies – especially food, raw materials and munitions – from the USA. The money that poured into the USA from Europe fuelled the growth of US industry and agriculture.
- Many countries also borrowed huge sums of money from the USA. American bankers and businessmen increasingly invested in Europe, and these investors made sizeable profits when the European economies recovered in the 1920s.
- During the war, European countries were unable to maintain their pre-war export levels. American manufacturers and farmers took over European overseas markets and expanded them further. For example, the USA replaced Germany as the world's leading producer of fertilisers and chemicals.

- The war stimulated technological advances, especially **mechanisation**, as well as the development of new raw materials, such as plastics. The USA led the world in new technology.

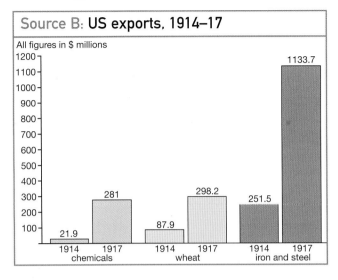

Source B: **US exports, 1914–17**

All figures in $ millions

presidency was cut short by his sudden death in 1923. Immediately after Harding died, it was revealed that he had been involved in financial scandals with close associates.

Coolidge, who succeeded Harding, carried on two of his predecessor's key policies: limiting the role of government in the economy and reducing the tax burden on the rich. Hoover, the millionaire president, was a self-made man. He was the Republicans' best example of what Americans could achieve with hard work and little government interference.

'The business of America is business'

President Coolidge made this statement in 1924. In the 1920s most Americans indeed believed that the government should be involved as little as possible in the day-to-day running of the economy. According to this view, if businessmen were left alone to make their own decisions, the result would be high profits, more jobs and good wages. This policy of limited government involvement in the economy was known as *laissez-faire*. Under this system, the government's role was to help business only when it was asked to.

Under Harding and Coolidge, the Republican economic policy of *laissez-faire* contributed to the prosperity of the USA. Low taxes and few regulations meant that businessmen were able to chase profits without fear of interference.

Successive Republican presidents also believed in 'rugged individualism'. This term was used by Hoover and other presidents who believed that people achieved success by their own hard work. It called to mind the courage and hardiness of the first western pioneers – those Americans who had journeyed to the West and made a new life for themselves in the wilderness.

Tasks

1. *What can you learn from Source A about immigration to the USA?*

2. *What can you learn from Source B about the effects of the First World War on the US economy?*

3. *Explain the effects of the First World War on the US economy. (For guidance on how to answer this type of question, see page 52.)*

4. *What can you learn from Source C about Republican attitudes to the economy?*

The policies of the Republican governments

In the 1920s the presidents of the USA were all Republicans. Therefore, they held similar political and economic views. They were:

- Warren Harding, 1921–23
- Calvin Coolidge, 1923–29
- Herbert Hoover, 1929–33

Harding, who took office in 1921, promised to take the USA '**back to normalcy**', but his

Source C: **From a speech given by Herbert Hoover in 1928**

During the war, we turned to the government to solve every difficult economic problem. When the Republican Party came to power, it restored the government to its position of umpire instead of a player. For these reasons the American people have gone forward in progress. Our opponents propose that we must thrust government into business. It would stifle initiative and invention.

Limited intervention

Nevertheless, the government of this period did act twice to intervene in the economy:

- The Fordney-McCumber **Tariff** (1922) raised **import duties** on goods coming into the USA to the highest level ever. This tariff thus protected American industry and encouraged Americans to buy home-produced goods.
- A reduction in income tax rates left some people with more cash to spend on **consumer goods**. Therefore, the market for home-produced items increased.

Technological change

The USA led the world in advances in technology. The development of electricity was fundamental to developments in technology. It provided a cheaper, more reliable and flexible form of power for factories and other industries. Moreover, it stimulated the production of associated electrical goods, such as refrigerators, vacuum cleaners and radios.

Other key developments included the conveyor belt and the **mass production** techniques adopted by the car industry (see page 16). These innovations speeded up industrial production, improved productivity and led to greater profits. New plastics, such as Bakelite, were used in household products. Glass tubing, automatic switchboards and concrete mixers all boosted American industry in various ways. New materials enabled the construction of new types of buildings. The skylines of America's great cities were gradually dotted with skyscrapers.

Consumerism

As profits increased, so did wages (though at nowhere near the same rate). Between 1923 and 1929, the average wage rose by 8 per cent. Though this was not a spectacular increase, it was enough to enable some workers to buy new consumer luxuries (see Source E). These goods were often bought on credit under a scheme known as hire purchase. The development of poster advertising (see Source F) and radio commercials encouraged people to buy these new goods.

At the start of the 1920s, the USA experienced another industrial revolution. One reason for this new revolution was the widespread use of electrical power. In 1912 only 16 per cent of Americans lived in electrically lit homes. By 1927 the number had risen to 63 per cent. The spread of electric power encouraged a much wider use of electrical goods, such as irons, ovens, washing machines, vacuum cleaners, refrigerators, radios and telephones. During this period, consumption of other energy sources also grew. Usage of oil doubled, and usage of gas quadrupled.

Source E: **Growth in sales of consumer goods**

	1919	Cars	1929
	9 million		26 million
	1920	Radios	1929
	60,000		10 million
	1915	Telephones	1930
	10 million		20 million
	1921	Refrigerators	1929
	For every one...		...there were 167

Source F: **Advert for a vacuum cleaner, 1920s**

Credit

The growth of credit schemes made it much easier for people to buy goods even when they did not have enough cash to pay for them immediately.

Source D: **An aerial view of New York's Wall Street and financial district, 1924**

Under the system of hire purchase, goods were paid for in instalments. About half the goods sold in the 1920s were paid for by hire purchase.

Confidence

Many Americans had confidence in their country's economy and were prepared to buy American goods, invest in American companies and try out new ideas. Indeed, most Americans believed that prosperity was not a privilege but a right. For many, the chief aim was to have a nice house filled with the latest consumer goods. Whereas in the past people had been encouraged to save and be **thrifty**, in the 1920s they were encouraged to 'spend, spend, spend'.

Isolationism

In the years after 1919, the USA returned to isolationism in its foreign policy. In particular, the government refused to become involved in political events in Europe. The isolationist mood also affected economic policy. The Republican governments placed tariffs on imported goods in order to limit foreign competition in the American marketplace. Imported goods became considerably more expensive than goods made in America. Therefore, people were encouraged to buy American goods, and US producers greatly benefited.

Tasks

5. *Study Source D. What were the key features of New York by the mid-1920s?*

6. *Describe the economic policies of the Republican governments of the 1920s. (For guidance on how to answer this type of question, see page 31.)*

7. *What can you learn from Source E about the US economy in the 1920s? (For guidance on how to answer this type of question, see page 26.)*

8. *There are several reasons for the economic boom of the 1920s, but which was the most important? Make a copy of the following grid. Give a rating for each factor, with a brief explanation for your choice. Decisive means the boom would not have happened without this factor. One example has been done for you.*

9. *What can you learn from Source F about advertisements in the USA in the 1920s?*

10. *Were the policies of the Republican governments of the 1920s the most important reason for the economic boom in the USA? Explain your answer.*

You may use the following information to help you with your answer:
- *The policies of the Republican governments*
- *The First World War*
- *Consumerism*
- *Credit and confidence*

(For guidance on how to answer this type of question, see page 119.)

	Quite important	Important	Decisive
Natural resources			
First World War			
Republican policy			
Consumerism			
Credit		Hire purchase encouraged people to buy more and increased demand.	
Confidence			
Cheap labour			
Technological change			
Isolationism			

Why was there a boom in the stock market?

The rise of the stock market

In the 1920s the stock market seemed to be the key to the prosperity of the USA. The value of stocks and shares rose steadily throughout the decade until 1928 and 1929, when they rose dramatically. The amount of buying and selling of shares grew substantially until it was a common occurrence for ordinary working people to become involved. The accepted image of the 1920s is that 'even the shoeshine boy' was dealing in shares.

Since shares in most companies seemed to rise in value, people were prepared to risk their money on buying shares. The USA began to speculate. Even if people did not have enough money to pay the full amount, they would make a deposit, borrow to pay the rest and then sell the shares in a couple of weeks when their value had risen and a profit had been made. The speculator would then pay off his debt and still have made money on the deal. (This process was called 'buying on the margin'.)

The number of shares traded in 1926 was about 451 million. The figure increased to 577 million the following year. By 1928, with share prices rising fast, there was a **bull market** on the Wall Street Stock Exchange, and in 1929, more than 1.1 billion shares were sold. Up to 25 million Americans became involved in the frenzy of share dealing in the last years of the decade. The graph below illustrates how quickly sales in shares grew.

Inside the New York Stock Exchange on Wall Street, 1925.

> **Source A:** **John J Raskob, a leading Democratic Party politician, speaking about the benefit of buying shares in 1928**
>
> *If a man saves $15 a week, and invests in good shares . . . at the end of twenty years [he] will have at least $80,000 and an income from investments of around $400 a month.*

> **Source B:** **From *After the Crash* by J Rublowsky, 1970, describing the share buying frenzy**
>
> *Almost any share was gobbled up in the hope of striking it rich but many of these were worthless. The Seaboard Airline was actually a railroad and had nothing to do with aviation, yet it attracted thousands of investors because aviation shares were the glamour issue of the day.*

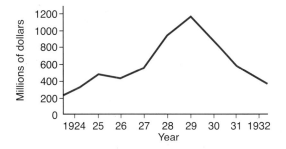

Graph showing sales of stocks and shares at the Wall Street Stock Exchange, 1923–32.

Source C: A view of speculation from *The Lawless Decade* by P Sann, 1957

Speculation wasn't gambling, it was an investment in the glorious American future, an expression of faith in the endless wondrous prosperity that blessed the land.

Source D: Shares being bought in a stockbroker's office on Wall Street in 1929

Tasks

1. What can you learn from Sources A and B about people who became involved in share dealing in the USA in the 1920s?

2. What does Source D suggest about the share boom?

3. Below is a concept map showing some reasons for the increase in selling/buying shares.

* *Copy the concept map and suggest other reasons for the increases by completing the blank boxes.*
* *Add new boxes or ones linked to those already there with more reasons.*

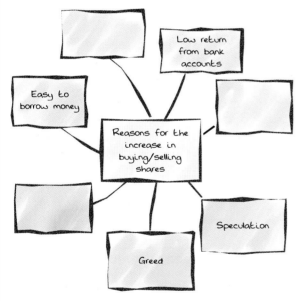

4. Explain why there was a boom in the stock market in the 1920s. (For guidance on how to answer this type of question, see page 74.)

5. What can you learn from Source C about speculation on the stock market? (For guidance on how to answer this type of question, see page 26.)

Speculation

Advice like that offered in Source A encouraged many Americans to invest in the stock market. Banks at the time were usually paying an annual interest rate of 7 per cent on savings accounts. The difference between the return on savings and the profit that could be made from speculation made the stock market an attractive gamble. The possibility of buying shares 'on the margin' fuelled speculation further.

Many investors borrowed money to buy shares. As long as share prices continued to rise, there was nothing to worry about. People were so confident about the market that by the summer of 1929, investors had borrowed a total of $8.5 billion to buy on the margin – a figure that had risen from $3.2 billion in 1926. The table below shows how consumer confidence increased the value of shares between 1928 and 1929.

Company	31 August 1928	3 September 1929	29 October 1929
American and Foreign Power	$38.00	$167.75	$73.00
AT and T	$182.00	$304.00	$230.00
Hershey Chocolate	$53.25	$128.00	$108.00
IBM	$130.86	$241.75	–
People's Gas, Chicago	$182.86	$182.86	–
Detroit Edison	$205.00	$350.00	–

Selected share prices, 1927–29. Why would these figures encourage people to buy shares *before* September 1929?

How important was the car industry?

The car industry played a very important role in the boom of the 1920s, often leading the way in technological change as well as stimulating the growth of other industries.

HENRY FORD

Henry Ford was an electrical engineer who built his first car in a rented brick shed. In 1909 he founded the Ford Motor Company in Detroit. In the same year he introduced his Model T Ford, which was nicknamed the 'tin lizzie'. Existing car manufacturers built several different models in a range of colours. Ford showed the benefits (and reduced costs) of manufacturing one standard model which was 'any colour as long as it was black'.

THE ASSEMBLY LINE

Ford introduced a much more efficient method of producing the cars – assembly line, or 'magic belt'. He had seen how efficiently this system was used in meat-packing factories and slaughterhouses. An electric conveyor belt carried the partly assembled car at a regular speed past workers who stood in the same spot and did one job, such as fitting on the wheels or doors. The worker did not have to waste time walking around fetching tools and equipment; tools and equipment were brought to him. As a result, a great deal of time was saved. In 1913 the Ford factory in Detroit was producing one car every three minutes. By 1920 the same factory was producing the same car model every ten seconds.

Source A: Henry Ford describes an assembly line in the mid-1920s

In the chassis assembly line there are 45 separate operations. Some men do only two small operations, others do more. The man who places the part does not fasten it. The man who puts the bolt in does not put the nut on and the man who puts the nut on does not tighten it. On operation 34 the motor gets its petrol. On operation 44 the radiator is filled with water and on operation 45 the car drives onto the road.

WORKFORCE

Ford believed in hard work. He would walk round his factory each day, encouraging his workers to do their job properly. However, he had quite a turnover of workers who found the assembly line boring and monotonous. Therefore, in 1914 Ford announced that he would double workers' wages to $5 – far more than any other employer paid for the equivalent job. Workers rushed to Detroit to work for him. He also reduced the length of the working day to eight hours and introduced a third shift, so that the factory was operating a three-shift system and operating 24 hours each day.

AFFORDABLE CARS

Ford's business methods and new technology allowed him to bring down the price of cars and thus make them affordable for many more Americans. In 1914 a Model T cost $850. By 1926 the price had dropped to $295. Ford also led the way in introducing hire purchase as a method of credit.

Source C: Henry Ford, speaking in 1921

It is better to sell a large number of cars at a reasonable small margin than to sell fewer cars at a larger margin of profit. I hold this because it enables a larger number of people to buy and enjoy the use of a car and because it gives a larger number of men employment at good wages.

ADVERTISING

Ford was also prepared to use modern advertising techniques to sell his cars. For example, he realised the value of using attractive women in adverts, not only because it would encourage men to buy his cars, but also to promote the idea of female drivers.

Source B: A Ford poster advert, 1923

Tasks

1. *What can you learn from Source A about the assembly line?*

2. *Study Source B. Put together your own advert for a Ford car.*

3. *Study Source C. Why does Ford suggest it is better to sell more cars?*

4. *Explain how Ford changed the car industry in the USA. (For guidance on how to answer this type of question, see page 84.)*

The impact of the Model T

Source D: **Model Ts on a high street in the USA in the mid-1920s**

Ford, more than anyone else, started an enormous growth in car ownership. By 1925 half the world's cars were Model Ts. In 1927 work was completed on a new Ford factory, the River Rouge complex, in Dearborn, Michigan. It became the biggest factory complex in the world and employed around 80,000 workers. By the late 1920s, Ford had established plants in Asia, Australia, Canada, South Africa and South America. His techniques were so effective that they were adopted by other US car manufacturers, as well as by Citroen and Renault in France and Morris and Austin in England.

Other benefits of the car industry

The car industry revolutionised American industry. Indeed it revolutionised American society:

- The car industry used so much steel, wood, petrol, rubber and leather that it provided jobs for more than five million people. By the late 1920s, cars and the car industry were using 90 per cent of the petrol, 80 per cent of the rubber and 75 per cent of the plate glass produced in the USA.
- Buying habits were transformed; hire purchase became a way of life for most Americans because it enabled an average family to buy a car.
- The car industry promoted road building and travel, and there was a knock-on effect on the leisure industry: hotels and restaurants were built in places that had been considered out of the way.

- It opened up the suburbs to more and more people who were now able to use the car to travel further to their place of work.
- Car ownership also benefited rural areas; the farmer, for example, could get to the local town in less than half an hour, and his wife no longer felt isolated in the farmhouse.
- Owning a car was no longer just a rich person's privilege, as it was in Europe in the mid-1920s. There was one car to every five people in the USA, one to 43 in Britain and one to 7000 in the Soviet Union.

The production of automobiles rose dramatically, from 1.9 million in 1920 to 4.5 million in 1929. The three main manufacturers were the giant firms of Ford, Chrysler and General Motors.

Tasks

5. *What does Source D suggest about the impact of the Model T?*

6. *Explain why the car industry benefited the USA in the 1920s. (For guidance on how to answer this type of question, see page 74.)*

7. *There were some Americans who opposed the growth of the car industry. What reasons might they have given at that time?*

Which other industries experienced a boom?

Although the car industry led the way, several other industries experienced a boom in the 1920s.

The construction industry

Economic growth led to a greater demand for buildings of every sort, including department stores, factories, houses in the suburbs, offices, hospitals and government buildings. There was a boom in office building as the number of banks, insurance and advertising companies and showrooms for new cars and electrical products grew rapidly. The development of new materials enabled the construction of new, taller types of buildings, which provided more space. The tallest buildings were skyscrapers, which transformed the skyline of New York and other major cities. More and more roads were needed as car sales soared. The American construction industry was busier in the 1920s than it had ever been before. Dependent industries also experienced a positive knock-on effect, and there was a growth in the manufacture of bricks, tiles, glass, furniture and electrical goods.

Source A: New York construction workers eat their lunches atop a steel beam 250 metres above ground, September 1932

Transport

The transport system improved greatly in the 1920s. By 1930 the total length of paved road in the USA had doubled, and the number of trucks on the road increased threefold to 3.5 million by 1929. Bus travel also proved popular. Air travel became possible for the first time in the 1920s. By 1929 there were 162,000 domestic and commercial flights. On 20 and 21 May 1927, Charles Lindbergh shot to world fame when he piloted the first non-stop solo transatlantic flight from New York to Paris in the single-seat, single-engine monoplane *Spirit of St Louis*. In the late 1920s and early 1930s, Lindbergh used his fame to promote the rapid development of US commercial aviation.

Source B: Charles Lindbergh, with *Spirit of St Louis* in background, May 31, 1927

Electricity and electrical goods

Electricity usage had developed slowly before the war but grew rapidly in the 1920s. By 1929 most homes in US cities had electricity. This stimulated industrial growth, as electricity provided a far more flexible and efficient form of power for factories and workshops. Moreover, it encouraged the development of a whole range of electrical goods, such as vacuum cleaners, radios, washing machines and refrigerators.

Source C: A table showing the growth in ownership of electrical goods in the 1920s

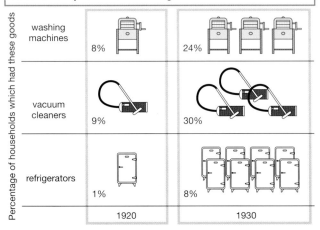

	1920	1930
washing machines	8%	24%
vacuum cleaners	9%	30%
refrigerators	1%	8%

Percentage of households which had these goods

Department stores

The 1920s also saw the growth of department stores as more and more people bought consumer goods, especially electrical appliances. In the cities, newly opened chain stores stocked the full range of goods that were now available. In addition, the USA was the first country to have a supermarket: JC Penney opened a chain of supermarkets known as Piggly Wiggly. The first was opened in Memphis, Tennessee, in 1916. Unlike in the old shops, where customers waited to be served at the shop counter, in the new shops customers helped themselves to the goods, which were individually priced, and paid for them at the checkout.

Source D: The inside of the first Piggly Wiggly store, 1918

Advertising

The advertising industry also grew rapidly as more and more firms realised the potential of advertisements for increasing sales and profits. The industry used sophisticated techniques incorporating eye-catching colour and memorable catch-phrases. Although magazines and newspapers remained the most important outlet, radio and cinema provided a range of new opportunities for advertisers.

Source E: Refrigerator advertisement from an American magazine, 1929

Tasks

1. *Study Source E. What methods are being used by the advertiser?*

2. *Describe the growth of two industries (apart from the car industry) in the USA during the 1920s. (For guidance on how to answer this type of question, see page 31.)*

3. *Create a mind map to show the growth of industries (include the car industry) during the 1920s. On your mind map, draw lines to link one industry to another. Write notes on the links about how growth in one industry could benefit another. For example, a line linking the car industry to construction would indicate that growth in the car industry encouraged road building.*

2 Declining industries

Task

What can you learn from Source A about the USA in 1928?

Chapter 1 discussed the economic boom the USA experienced in the 1920s. However, not all industries enjoyed the same sort of success. Indeed, some faced shrinking markets and new challenges. Workers in the railway, textile and coal-mining industries, for example, faced unemployment and low wages. Some found their working hours shortened, and others even had to work longer hours for less pay. There was much resentment among the workers in these industries, who received little help until the **New Deal** in the 1930s. (The unique problems faced by the agriculture industry are dealt with in Chapter 3.)

This chapter answers the following questions:

• Why did the coal industry face problems in the 1920s?
• How did the railroad industry suffer?
• What challenges did the textiles industry face?

Examination skills

This chapter gives guidance on question 1a from Unit 2. This question, which is worth four marks, is a source inference question.

Why did the coal industry face problems in the 1920s?

Just as the 'new' industries of the 1920s experienced several years of boom, so the 'old' industries faced a period of decline. One of the most important industries was coal, which had provided the base for America's industrial revolution. However, as the use of oil and its derivatives became more widespread, coal producers found it difficult to compete. To make matters worse, coal faced further competition from gas and electricity, which were becoming more widely used.

In the early 1920s, there were about 12,000 mines and more than 700,000 miners in the USA. A great many mines closed down during the 1920s, and many thousands of miners were made redundant.

As the demand for coal fell, employers did not always sack the miners. One solution was to have them work fewer hours each day. There were many strikes across the mining regions in order to secure decent wages and improved working conditions, but these strikes were rarely successful. In some cases, police officers and state troops were used against the strikers.

Some mine owners did not allow their workers to join a **trade union**. For these workers, it was therefore impossible to strike. Other owners employed only non-union workers. Those mines where there were no union members were able to keep up the supply.

Most miners, especially in the Appalachian Mountains (in the eastern United States), did not look for employment elsewhere and accepted the reduction in their standard of living. By 1929 the average wage of a coal-miner was about $100. By contrast, the average wage of a bricklayer in New York was more than $300 per month. Thus the coal-miner had not really been able to share in the prosperity of the decade.

Source A: **Two striking miners from Pennsylvania seek support and monetary contributions in New York in December 1927**

Task

What can you learn from Source A about the coal industry in the 1920s?

How did the railroad industry suffer?

The second 'old' industry to suffer in the 1920s was the railroad industry. Owing to the huge growth of car ownership in the 1920s, the volume of passenger traffic on the railroads declined quickly. The rapid development of a nationwide road network, together with the availability of cheap cars and cheap petrol, presented a very serious challenge to the railroad companies. It was a challenge they could not meet. The railroad companies in some of the larger cities, where electric railways had been built just before 1914, fared particularly badly.

Companies did increase their carrying of freight in the 1920s by about 10 per cent, but this increase would have been far greater had it not been for the expansion of road traffic. Few railroad companies made large profits during this period.

Task

Why were the railroads unable to prosper in the 1920s?

Trams and cars fill Times Square, in the centre of New York, in this photograph from around 1925.

What challenges did the textiles industry face?

For a number of reasons, the textiles industry also experienced many problems during the 1920s.

Tariffs

Since 1913, when tariffs on wool and cotton had been lowered, the US textiles industry had had to face foreign competition. There were some adjustments to the tariffs in the 1920s, but they were not significant enough to restore the situation to the way it had been before 1913.

Rayon

The textile industry faced the challenge of a new product – rayon. This man-made fibre was far cheaper to produce than wool, cotton or silk. Rayon required less processing and fewer workers than natural fibres. It was 50 per cent cheaper than silk. Rayon was used initially for men's socks and later for lingerie and dresses. Its most common use was for women's stockings.

Rayon production increased from 4.5 million kg in 1920 to 50 million kg by the end of the 1920s.

Fashion

One of the most important reasons why textiles suffered in the 1920s was dramatic change in women's fashion. By the end of the First World War, women's dresses were much shorter than they had been in 1914, and new trends in the 1920s shortened them even more. An average dress needed about seven metres of material in 1928. Before the war, it had needed almost three times that amount.

Impact on workers

Because of these challenges facing the industry, owners of textiles factories looked for ways of making production cheaper. For example, they adopted the new techniques of scientific management, which were being used in other industries. Owners employed industrial efficiency consultants to find ways of getting more work out of each employee. Those owners who could afford it invested in new machinery, and workers were sacked as a result.

In the southern states, mill owners kept wages low by employing children or women. Southern owners were helped by the **Supreme Court**, which declared that two states that had banned child labour had acted **unconstitutionally**. Statutes outlawing child labour were removed. Moreover, the Supreme Court stepped in to ban laws which set **minimum wages** for women. Therefore, textile mills in the North (in Massachusetts, for example) either closed down or moved south, where labour was cheap. In the late 1920s, the average mill wage in the South was about $13 for a 60-hour week. One result of low wages was an increase in the number of strikes in the industry during the 1920s.

Two women in fashionable short dresses dance the Charleston in Washington, DC, in 1925. In front of them is a politician from Charleston, South Carolina.

Source A: Striking textile workers in Passaic, New Jersey, in 1926. Police can be seen attacking some strikers and their families, and there are children on the ground

Source B: An extract from the song 'Cotton Mill Colic' by Dave McCarn (1905–64), a mill worker and folk singer from North Carolina. The song was written in 1926

When you go to work you work like the devil,
At the end of the week you're not on the level
Payday comes, you pay your rent,
When you get through you've not got a cent
To buy fat-back meat, pinto beans,
Now and then you get turnip greens.
No use to colic, we're all that way,
Can't get the money to move away.
I'm a-gonna starve, and everybody will,
'Cause you can't make a living at a cotton mill.

Twelve dollars a week is all we get,
How in the heck can we live on that?
I've got a wife and fourteen kids,
We all have to sleep on two bedsteads.
Patches on my britches, holes in my hat,
Ain't had a shave, my wife got fat.
No use to colic, everyday at noon,
The kids get to crying in a different tune.
I'm a-gonna starve, and everybody will,
'Cause you can't make a living at a cotton mill.

Tasks

1. Re-read pages 19–23 and study Source A. Why were strikes unsuccessful in the 'old' industries?

2. In what ways does Source B help you to understand the problems of the workers in the textile industry in the 1920s?

3. Copy and complete the table below, placing the problems each industry faced in order of importance.

Problems for the coal industry	Problems for the textiles industry	Problems for the railroad industry

4. Working in groups of three or four, write a song highlighting the problems of the workers in the 'old' industries in the 1920s.

Examination practice

This section provides guidance on how to answer question 1a from Unit 2, which is worth four marks. This is the source inference question.

Question 1 – source inference

What does Source A tell us about wages in the textile mills in the USA? (4 marks)

How to answer

- You are being asked to give the message or messages of the source, to read between the lines of what is written.
- In addition, you must support the inference. In other words, use details from the source to support the messages you say it gives.
- Begin your answer with 'The source suggests…'
- Look for key words in the source that might lead to inferences. You could tackle this by copying the source and highlighting different messages in different colours to help identify messages (as in the example below).
- Avoid repeating the content of the source.
- For maximum marks you will need to make at least two supported references. For example, in Source A two messages could be:

Inference
The source suggests that wages were inadequate.

Support from the source
The writer indicates that the workers only just had enough money for food and clothes.

> **Source A**
>
> Some of the older industries in the USA suffered from competition and could not pay high wages. The workers in the textiles industry complained that they barely earned enough to buy food and clothes. Saving was out of the question. There were no treats or outings.

Inference
Source A suggests that low pay meant a hard life, that people worked just to live.

Support from the source
The writer points out that people could not save money or make life less harsh by treating themselves.

> **Source A: From a history of the USA published in 2002**
>
> *Some of the older industries in the USA suffered from competition and could not pay high wages. The workers in the textiles industry complained that they barely earned enough to buy food and clothes. Saving was out of the question. There were no treats or outings.*

Now have a go yourself

Try answering question 2 using the steps shown for question 1.

> **Source B: From a history of the USA published in 1999**
>
> *Many view the USA in the 1920s as a country of great wealth. This is only part of the picture. There were many poor people and not all industries experienced a boom. Thousands of black Americans who worked in the textile industry left the South to seek jobs in the North. However, it was not only textiles which suffered; unemployment in the coal industry rose quickly during this period.*

Question 2 – source inference

What does Source B tell us about industries in the USA in the 1920s? (4 marks)

3 Problems in agriculture

Source A: A cartoon of the 1920s depicting the difficult times faced by American farmers

FARM FOR SALE

Task

What message is the cartoonist trying to put across?

Agriculture in the USA experienced fluctuating fortunes during the first thirty years of the twentieth century. In general, farmers saw profits rise until the early 1920s because of increased demand – from within their own country and also from the wider world. But after the initial post-war boom, farmers experienced severe economic problems. The 1920s was a decade of contrasts in the USA. There were pockets of poverty amid the vast wealth, and agriculture was a good example of this phenomenon. The average wage of a farm worker was far lower than that of an industrial worker in the northern states. Some farmers had to sell their homes and became tenants on what had been their own land. By the end of the decade, thousands of farmers were unemployed. Yet farmers in California and Florida enjoyed a period of prosperity throughout the 1920s.

This chapter answers the following questions:

• Why did agriculture experience a period of prosperity before 1920?
• Why was there overproduction in agriculture in the USA?
• Why did many agricultural workers become unemployed in the 1920s?

Examination skills

This chapter gives guidance on question 1b from Unit 2. This question, which is worth six marks, is a describe question. It usually asks you to describe the key features of actions or events in a given period.

Why did agriculture experience a period of prosperity before 1920?

During the first two decades of the twentieth century, farmers in the USA enjoyed a period of rising profits. At this time, about 30 million people were employed in the farming industry – either directly, by working on the land, or indirectly, by working in associated businesses, such as fertiliser production. During the First World War, improvements in the standard of living had led to a rise in the demand for food. Exports to Europe had also increased because supplies to some markets from Britain and France had been cut off.

In response to the growth in their industry, farmers cultivated land which had not been used before. In the post-war boom, farmers ploughed an additional eight million hectares of hitherto unfarmed land. Some returning soldiers saw agriculture as a way of making money quickly and borrowed heavily to purchase land and machinery.

In 1917 Henry Ford developed the Fordson tractor, which sold more than 750,000 in its first ten years of production. The tractor enabled farmers to become more efficient and produce more crops, especially wheat and corn. This in turn increased demand for the combine harvester, used to reap the crops (although this machine had been in widespread use for some time). The combine harvester, which was not used in Europe, gave American farmers an advantage over their international competitors.

American farmers produced more food than the USA needed, but this was not a problem while the world bought American foodstuffs. Continuing prosperity depended on farmers maintaining their foreign markets. However, by the end of 1920, agriculture was beginning to experience distinct problems.

Source B: **A combine harvester at work in Walla Walla, Washington state, around 1902**

Source A: **Fordson tractor sold by Parkway Motor Co. of Washington, DC, around 1921**

Task

Look at Sources A and B. List the advantages and disadvantages of the use of these machines for farmers and their labourers.

Why was there overproduction in agriculture in the USA?

At the beginning of the 1920s, demand in Europe for American agricultural produce was beginning to decline as Europe began to return to economic stability. President Wilson tried to help the farmers by introducing the Emergency Tariff Act (1921). This act increased **import duties** on wheat, sugar, meat, wool and other agricultural products from abroad and thus gave American producers of those goods some protection in the domestic market.

The USA also faced stronger competition from other European industries during the brief post-war boom. The US government responded by introducing the Fordney McCumber Act (1922). This act allowed tariffs to be increased on goods coming into the USA. One unintended consequence was the retaliation abroad – many countries placed similar tariffs on goods from the USA, including agricultural produce. As a result, US farmers saw the price of their own produce increase abroad, and they thus became less competitive. In addition, wheat production in Canada, Argentina and Australia provided an extremely serious challenge to US farmers.

In order to maintain their livelihood, farmers could do little else than continue to produce food and try to sell it at a lower price. One solution would have been a general reduction in levels of production, but any farmer reducing his output was taking a large risk: how could he be sure that all the other farmers would do the same?

Consequently, overproduction continued. It was ironic that as farmers became more mechanised and more efficient, they produced more food – and this success drove prices down and this provided them with less income.

The Agricultural Credits Act (1923) was introduced to try to solve the problems in the farming sector. The act established twelve Federal Intermediate Credit Banks, which were allowed to lend money to farmers. This move did help some farmers, but the new credit measures did not really address the most pressing farming issue: over-production. Some farmers were already having to sell up and deal with unemployment.

In 1924 **Congress** did try to help farmers by introducing the McNary-Haugen Farm Relief Bill. This bill sought to create a Federal Farm Board which would:

- buy any agricultural surpluses at 1914 prices
- store surpluses until demand returned in the USA or until the global markets became more favourable.

The bill was **vetoed** by President Coolidge; as a supporter of *laissez-faire,* he opposed too much government interference in any industry. The farmers' problems were not being solved, and more and more of them were facing the prospect of unemployment.

Tasks

1. *Why did the USA face foreign competition after 1918?*

2. *Describe US government policies towards agriculture after the First World War. (For guidance on how to answer this type of question, see page 31.)*

3. *Study Sources A and B on page 26 and re-read the text on pages 26 and 27. Construct a spider diagram which shows why there was agricultural overproduction in the 1920s.*

4. *Why did US farmers fail to reduce agricultural output?*

Why did many agricultural workers become unemployed in the 1920s?

As well as foreign competition, American farmers faced numerous problems at home. Some issues affected all farmers and others touched specific sectors of agriculture. These problems led to financial crisis for many farmers. Prosperity ended, and there was widespread unemployment in many states. The diagram at the bottom of the page explains the issues farmers faced during the 1920s.

Despite the profits some farmers made, those who owned only small amounts of land experienced the greatest problems. Even in 1920, there were more than three million farmers who earned less than $1000 per annum. This figure was seen as the minimum a family required. A farm labourer's income – even in the most affluent years of the 1920s – was only about half of a coal-miner's income, and little more than one-quarter of a clerical worker's. Farmers were among the poorest paid workers in the USA and were the first to be hit by the economic problems of the late 1920s. By then, in parts of the South farm labourers were earning only about $50 per month, whereas a skilled manufacturing worker was earning $140.

Many farmers borrowed money simply to pay their mortgage. When all avenues of credit were exhausted, they had to surrender their land and home to the banks and found themselves unemployed for the first time. Some small farmers even re-mortgaged their land. When mortgages were eventually foreclosed, some farmers remained as tenants or moved to the cities, where they hoped to get work. Some even became **sharecroppers** (a sharecropper was a tenant farmer who gave a share of his crops as rent). In 1924 alone, more than 600,000 farmers went bankrupt. Some workers even moved to California to find work on the successful fruit farms. It has been estimated that about one million black farm workers became unemployed during the 1920s.

The 1920s was the first time in US history that the total number of farm workers began to shrink. Farmers borrowed more than $2 billion in order to keep hold of their property, but often it was difficult to borrow because some banks did not see farmers as a good risk.

Source A: **Selected US farm prices, 1917–25**			
Year	Cattle per head ($)	Cotton per 500 grams (cents)	Wheat per bushel ($)
1919	54.65	35.34	2.16
1920	52.64	15.89	1.83
1921	39.07	17.00	1.03
1922	30.09	22.88	0.97
1923	31.66	28.69	0.93
1924	32.11	22.91	1.25
1925	31.72	19.61	1.44

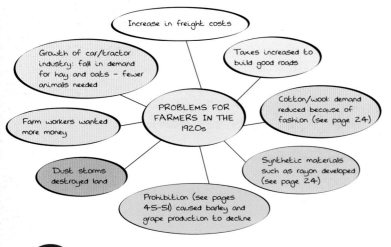

Spider diagram: PROBLEMS FOR FARMERS IN THE 1920s
- Increase in freight costs
- Growth of car/tractor industry: fall in demand for hay and oats – fewer animals needed
- Taxes increased to build good roads
- Cotton/wool: demand reduced because of fashion (see page 24)
- Farm workers wanted more money
- Synthetic materials such as rayon developed (see page 24)
- Dust storms destroyed land
- Prohibition (see pages 45–51) caused barley and grape production to decline

Tasks

1. *Study the spider diagram on the left. Suggest reasons why each problem was harmful to farmers in the 1920s.*

2. *What can you learn from Source A about the problems faced by farmers in the 1920s?*

3. *Explain how farmers tried to tackle the problems they faced in the 1920s. (For guidance on how to answer this type of question, see page 93.)*

Examination practice

This section provides guidance on how to answer question 1b from Unit 2, which is worth six marks. There is further guidance on how to answer this type of question on page 44.

Question 1 – describe

Describe the successes US farmers experienced in the years to 1920. (6 marks)

How to answer

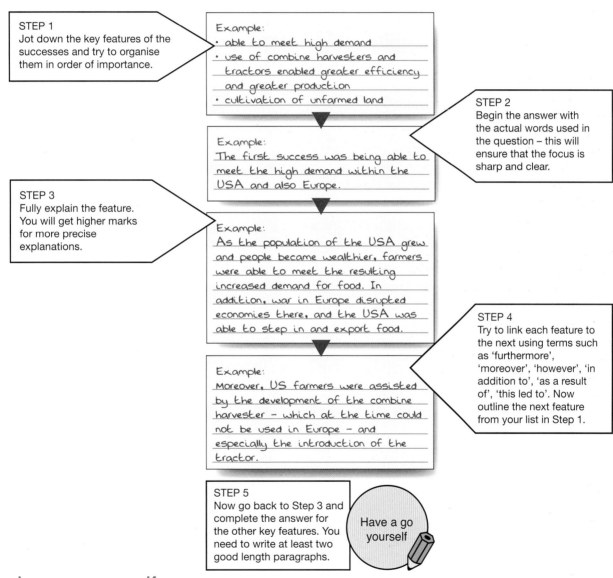

STEP 1
Jot down the key features of the successes and try to organise them in order of importance.

Example:
- able to meet high demand
- use of combine harvesters and tractors enabled greater efficiency and greater production
- cultivation of unfarmed land

STEP 2
Begin the answer with the actual words used in the question – this will ensure that the focus is sharp and clear.

Example:
The first success was being able to meet the high demand within the USA and also Europe.

STEP 3
Fully explain the feature. You will get higher marks for more precise explanations.

Example:
As the population of the USA grew and people became wealthier, farmers were able to meet the resulting increased demand for food. In addition, war in Europe disrupted economies there, and the USA was able to step in and export food.

STEP 4
Try to link each feature to the next using terms such as 'furthermore', 'moreover', 'however', 'in addition to', 'as a result of', 'this led to'. Now outline the next feature from your list in Step 1.

Example:
Moreover, US farmers were assisted by the development of the combine harvester – which at the time could not be used in Europe – and especially the introduction of the tractor.

STEP 5
Now go back to Step 3 and complete the answer for the other key features. You need to write at least two good length paragraphs.

Have a go yourself

Now have a go yourself

Try answering question 2 using the steps shown above for question 1.

2. Describe the problems farmers faced in the USA in the 1920s. (6 marks)

Key Topic 2: US society 1919–29

Source A: **A photo, taken in 1926, of a black man who has been lynched**

Source B: 'Strange Fruit' was written by Lewis Allan and sung most famously by Billie Holiday, an African American blues singer. The haunting song describes a lynching

Southern trees bear a strange fruit
Blood on the leaves and blood at the root
Black bodies swinging in the southern breeze
Strange fruit hanging from the poplar trees.
Pastoral scene of the gallant south,
The bulging eyes and the twisted mouth;
And the sudden smell of burning flesh.
Here is the fruit for the crows to pluck,
For the rain to gather, for the wind to suck,
For the sun to rot, for the tree to drop,
Here is a strange and bitter crop.

Tasks

1. *Study Source B. What is the song's message? Which line do you think is the most effective?*

2. *Study Sources A and B. What impression do they give you of US society in the 1920s?*

This key topic examines the main features of the roaring twenties, including **consumerism**, new forms of entertainment, the impact of the cinema and changes in the position of women, especially the **flappers**. It also explains the reasons for and the social effects of Prohibition, in particular the rise of organised crime and the activities of Al Capone and other gangsters. The final chapter highlights intolerance and racism in the USA in the 1920s. It examines attitudes to immigrants and black Americans and the activities of the Ku Klux Klan. Furthermore it shows the importance of two key trials, the 'Monkey Trial' and Sacco and Vanzetti.

Each chapter explains a key issue and examines important lines of enquiry as outlined below:

Chapter 4 The roaring twenties (pages 33–44)

- What was meant by 'consumerism'?
- In what ways did the position of women change?
- What new forms of entertainment were there?
- What was meant by the 'jazz age'?

Chapter 5 Prohibition and gangsters (pages 45–52)

- Why was Prohibition introduced?
- What effects did it have on US society?
- Why was there an increase in organised crime?

- What was the importance of gangsters such as Capone?

Chapter 6 Racism and intolerance (pages 53–65)

- What was the attitude towards immigrants and immigration?
- Why was the Sacco and Vanzetti case important?
- What was the Ku Klux Klan?
- What was the experience of black Americans in the 1920s?
- What was the Monkey trial?

The roaring twenties

Source A: A queue outside a cinema in 1925	Source B: From a newspaper article written in the mid-1920s

Source B:

Jazz employs primitive rhythms which excite the baser human instincts. Jazz music also causes drunkenness. Reason and reflection are lost and the actions of the persons are directed by the stronger animal passions.

Task

What can you learn from Sources A and B about life in the USA in the 1920s?

There were rapid social changes in the USA in the 1920s, and the period is often referred to as the 'roaring twenties'. These changes included a growth in demand for **consumer goods** and a transformation in the status of some women, especially those known as the flappers. Radio and the cinema revolutionised entertainment. Hollywood, in California, became the centre of the film industry. More and more people watched and participated in sport. Modern forms of music, such as jazz, and dances such as the Charleston, became popular.

This chapter answers the following questions:

• What was meant by 'consumerism?'
• In what ways did the position of women change?
• What new forms of entertainment were there?
• What was meant by the 'jazz age'?

Examination skills

This chapter gives additional guidance on answering question 1b from Unit 2. This question, which is worth six marks, is a key-features describe question.

What was meant by 'consumerism'?

The growth in female employment (see page 38) also increased the need for labour-saving devices, such as washing machines and vacuum cleaners.

Hire purchase schemes (see page 13) made it easier to buy goods on **credit**.

Owing to the spread in popular entertainment, more and more Americans bought radios.

By 1927 two-thirds of US homes had electricity. This situation stimulated the demand for electrical goods, such as washing machines and vacuum cleaners.

For the majority of workers in industry, wages increased. Between 1923 and 1929, the average wage rose by 8 per cent. In other words, workers had more spare money to spend on consumer goods.

The economic boom of the 1920s was fuelled partly by the growth of consumerism, the growing demand among many Americans for everyday items, often household goods. As the diagram above shows, the increased demand for consumer goods was due to several factors.

The impact of the motor car

The clearest example of 1920s consumerism was the boom in the car industry. Chapter 1 gave an explanation of the effect the assembly line had on the growth of the car industry (see pages 16–18). Above all else, Henry Ford made the car affordable.

Source A: From an article in the New York *Daily Tribune*, 1929

Any American willing to get up early enough can look out of his own windows and see a trail of thousands of workmen's automobiles scooting down the boulevards to the factory or new building destination. Even ten years ago this great mass of labour had to live just around the corner in a hovel next to the factory or hang on street cars at six o'clock in the morning in order to reach the building site.

Advertising

The importance of advertising was explained in Chapter 1 (see pages 12, 17 and 20). Designers of advertisements studied the psychology of consumers and devised methods which they believed would encourage people to buy the products. Women were used to advertise many goods. Women were also important targets for the advertisers.

Source B: The manager of an advertising firm explains how to appeal to women

Nine-tenths of the goods bought annually are bought by women. Woman is a creature of the imagination. We pay her a compliment when we say this, for imagination comes from the feelings and feelings come from the heart. And so the advertising appeal, to reach women, must not ignore the first great quality of the heart, which is love. Most advertisers do not ignore the quality of love. There, in almost every advertisement, is a reference, in word or picture, to mother love, to the home, to children, to sentiment.

Tasks

1. *Explain why consumerism grew in the USA in the 1920s. (For guidance on how to answer this type of question, see page 74.)*

2. *What can you learn from Source A about the impact of the motor car?*

3. *Study Source B. In what ways did advertisers try to appeal to women?*

In what ways did the position of women change?

The position of women before 1917

POLITICAL POSITION
Women played no part in politics. They did not have the vote.

SOCIAL POSITION
It was thought to be un-ladylike to smoke or drink in public. A woman would be accompanied by a **chaperone** if she went out during the day or evening. Divorce was rare, and so was sex before marriage.

EMPLOYMENT
Opportunities were limited. Most middle- and upper-class women did not go out to work as this would interfere with their domestic role as mother and housewife. Most working women were employed in low paid jobs, such as cleaning, dress-making and secretarial work.

APPEARANCE
Women were expected to wear tight-waisted, ankle-length dresses, have long hair which was tied back and to wear no make-up.

Source A: **Elementary schoolgirls learning to cook, Washington, DC, 1900**

Changes after 1917

After 1917, several factors changed the position of women – especially a group known as the flappers.

- The USA's entry into the First World War provided new employment opportunities for women, especially in heavy industry. They proved they could do these jobs just as well as men. This sort of work also encouraged freer behaviour. For the first time, women smoked and drank in public and went out unchaperoned.
- Women were given the vote in 1920. This increase in political power encouraged some to campaign for further change.
- During the consumer boom of the 1920s, the development of new labour-saving devices, such as vacuum cleaners and washing machines, gave women more opportunities for leisure and work.

Tasks

1. *What image does Source A give of the life of American women in 1900?*

2. *Describe the position of women in the USA in the early twentieth century.*
   (Remember how to answer this type of question? For further guidance, see page 31.)

3. *Explain why the position of women changed after 1917.*
   (For guidance on how to answer this type of question, see page 74.)

The flappers

In the 1920s a number of women, generally from middle- and upper-class families living in the northern states, decided to challenge society's traditional attitudes towards women. They became known as the flappers. Their aim was to become more independent in their social life and to take a freer approach to their behaviour and appearance.

They cut their hair short and wore make-up.

They wore short skirts and very bright clothes.

They openly danced with men in public. Their particular favourite was the new craze, the Charleston. They also listened to controversial new music known as jazz.

They smoked and drank in public.

They drove cars and even motorbikes.

They went out to speakeasies and to the cinema without a chaperone.

They wore very revealing swimming costumes on public beaches.

Source B: Flappers dance the Charleston at a New York club in 1926

Source C: F Scott Fitzgerald was a famous American author who wrote about the roaring twenties. In 1920 he married Zelda Zayre, who was a typical flapper

Flirting, kissing, viewing life lightly, saying damn without a blush, playing along the danger line in an immature way – a sort of mental baby vamp.

Source D: An article with the title 'Flapper Jane' from a US magazine, 1925

Jane's a flapper. Let us take a look at the young person as she strolls across the lawn of her parent's suburban home, having just put the car away after driving sixty miles in two hours. She is, for one thing, a pretty girl. Beauty is the fashion in 1925. She is frankly, heavily made up with poisonously scarlet lips and richly ringed eyes. As for her clothes, Jane isn't wearing much this summer. Her dress is brief. It is cut low. The skirt comes just below the knees. The bra has been abandoned since 1924.

Source E: From a letter written to the *Daily Illini*, 1922

The word 'flapper' to us means not a female that smokes, swears and kisses her gentlemen friends goodnight, although there is no harm in any of that. We think of the flapper as the independent young woman who feels like punching someone when called the 'weaker sex', who resents being put on a pedestal and who is responsible for the advancement of women's condition in the world.

In some respects, however, the flappers did not advance the cause of women's rights in the 1920s. Many traditional groups, especially in rural areas, saw them as too extreme, and they met with strong disapproval from religious societies. Some flappers deliberately flouted the law and were arrested – for example, for wearing revealing clothing such as banned swimsuits (see Source F). Other observers dismissed the flappers as simply pleasure-seeking women with few other attributes.

Source F: A group of flappers in Chicago being arrested for wearing banned one-piece bathing suits which were seen as too figure-hugging

Source G: An English journalist writing about flappers in the USA in 1921

Think of the modern young American girl of this great country. Do they ever think? Do they ever ask whence they have come? It would seem not. Their aim appears to be to attract men and to secure money. What can a man with a mind find to hold him in one of these lovely, brainless, cigarette-smoking creatures of undisciplined sex whom he meets continually?

Tasks

4. Study all the sources on these two pages. Then copy and complete the following table. An example has been done for you.

Source	Positive features of flappers	Negative features
D		Interested only in their appearance

5. Overall, do you think the flappers improved the status of women? Explain your answer.

Other changes in the position of women

There were other important developments in the status of women in the USA in the 1920s.

Employment opportunities

There was certainly progress in the numbers of women in employment. By 1930 two million more women were employed than had been the case ten years earlier. However, these women tended to do poorly paid unskilled jobs. Despite the fact that a third of university degrees were awarded to women in 1930, only 4 per cent of university professors were women. Medical schools allocated only 5 per cent of places to women. Consequently, the number of female doctors actually declined in the 1920s.

A man doing the same job as a woman still received a lot more pay. Women received no support from the **Supreme Court**, which banned all attempts to set **minimum wages** for women. In 1927, when female textile workers in Tennessee went on strike for better pay, the government took the side of the employers. The strikers were arrested by the local police.

There were some new career opportunities for women, but these were in so-called 'women's jobs', such as librarians and nurses.

Source H: A table showing the percentage of women in certain jobs in the years 1900–30		
	1900	1930
Professional and technical workers	8	14
Managers and officials	1	3
Clerical and sales workers	8	28
Skilled craftspeople	1	1
Workers and labourers	26	19
Domestic servants	29	18
Other service workers	7	10
Farmers	6	2

Marriage

The media, and especially magazines, reminded women that they should marry and have children. Once women married, they generally gave up work. Nevertheless, married women in the 1920s tended to have fewer children and lived longer than their mothers and grandmothers had. In 1900, the average lifespan for a woman was 51 years. By 1925 this figure had increased to 63. In 1900, American women had an average of 3.6 children. This figure had fallen to 2.6 by 1930.

Women were less likely to remain in unhappy marriages in the 1920s. In 1914 there were 100,000 divorces. There were twice as many in 1929.

Politics

Women were given the vote in 1920. A few women did make progress in gaining political power. For example, in 1924 Nellie Tayloe Ross of Wyoming became the first woman to be elected **governor** of a state. Two years later, Bertha Knight Landes became the first female mayor of an American city, Seattle.

However, these women were the exception, and women made little progress in politics itself. Political parties wanted their vote but did not see them as realistic candidates for political office. By 1920 there were only a handful of female politicians. Most women, in any case, had little interest in politics. The **women's movement** failed in its attempt to get the Equal Rights Amendment Act passed. The act would have given women equality in law with men.

Entertainment

The popularity of the cinema, radio and dance halls provided further opportunities for women. For example, Mary Pickford and Clara Bow became stars of silent movies; they were so successful that they joined two other stars in setting up their own film company. Mae West, Gloria Swanson and Jean Harlow became stars of the 'talkies' and role models for many younger American girls.

Society

The flappers did pave the way for a more tolerant approach to the social position of women. More women worked, and with more money of their own, working women increasingly made the decisions about whether to buy new items for the home. Even women who did not earn their own money were increasingly seen as the ones who took these purchasing decisions. Advertising was aimed specifically at women for this reason. It has even been suggested that it was pressure from women that convinced Ford to offer other colours, apart from black, for their cars.

In addition, the new labour-saving devices such as vacuum cleaners, released women from some of the time previously spent on domestic chores. This enabled some to go into employment and provided others with more opportunity for leisure and recreational activities.

However, there was still a strong conservative element in US society – especially in rural areas, where religion and traditional attitudes prevented any real change.

Many married women could not afford the new labour-saving devices. A survey in 1932 of 10,000 farmhouses found that only 32 per cent had any running water at all, with 57 per cent owning a washing machine. Only 47 per cent had carpet sweepers. These women not only spent a considerable time on housework and looking after the children, they also had to milk the cows and work in the fields. They experienced little change and few benefits from the roaring twenties.

Source J: Written by Doris E Fleischman and published in *America as Americans See It* (1932)

It is wholly confusing to read the advertisements in the magazines that feature the enticing qualities of vacuum cleaners, refrigerators and hundreds of other devices which should lighten the chores of women in the home. On the whole these large middle classes do their own housework with few of the mechanical aids. Women who live on farms do a great deal of work besides caring for their children, washing the clothes and caring for the home and cooking. Thousands still work in the fields and help milk the cows.

Tasks

6. *What can you learn from Source J about women in rural areas of the USA in the 1920s and early 1930s?*

7. *Study Source I. Give two examples of progress for women from this advert.*

8. *Working in pairs, make a copy of the following set of scales.*

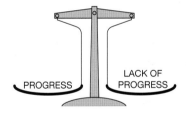

PROGRESS   LACK OF PROGRESS

Using evidence from pages 33–37,

- *one of the pair write examples of progress on the left-hand scale*
- *the other write examples of lack of progress on the right-hand scale.*

9. *Overall, do you think women made progress in their position in US society in the 1920s? Give reasons for your answer.*

10. *Explain the effects that the roaring twenties had on the position of women in the USA. (For guidance on how to answer this type of question, see page 52.)*

What new forms of entertainment were there?

In the USA in the 1920s, there was a growth in the popularity of many forms of entertainment, including sport, radio and the cinema. Labour-saving devices for the home, like washing machines, gave people more free time. **Mass production** meant people worked less. Americans began to look for ways to fill their spare time, especially as many were now better paid. They wanted to forget about the war and set out to enjoy themselves. A whole pleasure industry grew up, giving Americans new entertainments to spend their money on. The boom of the 1920s brought new forms of music and dance as well as increased popularity for spectator sports.

NEWSPAPERS AND MAGAZINES

More and more people bought newspapers and magazines. In 1919 the first tabloid newspaper, the *Daily News*, was published. This breakthrough encouraged other publications, which concentrated on crime, cartoon strips and fashion. People wanted to read about heroes and heroines of sport and cinema. Advertisers were keen to use magazines and newspapers to sell their goods. In 1922, ten magazines each claimed a circulation of over 2.5 million.

Source A: The heavyweight boxing champion Gene Tunney sends Jack Dempsey to the canvas in the eighth round of their 1927 title bout in Chicago

SPORT

In the early 1920s sport became a very important part of the lives of many Americans. The radio made following major sports events even more popular. Indeed, the 1920s was officially named the 'Golden Age of Sport'. Baseball, football, horse racing and tennis captured the imagination of many people. Baseball was the most popular game; Babe Ruth, the most popular sportsman of the time, had a major influence on the younger generation because he was not shy about drinking and smoking in public.

Spectators flocked to see sporting events. In 1924, 67,000 watched the football match between Illinois and Michigan in the Memorial Stadium. In 1927, some 145,000 saw the boxing match between Jack Dempsey and Gene Tunney.

THE CINEMA

The most popular form of entertainment in the 1920s was the movies. A visit to the cinema became an integral part of American life.

By 1926 there were over 17,000 movie houses, including many in small villages. Until 1927 there was no soundtrack on films. A pianist played tunes while the film ran. He would play fast music for chase scenes and romantic music for love scenes. The film stars of the silent era included Charlie Chaplin and Greta Garbo. In 1926 it was reported that Greta Garbo earned $5000 a week.

Rudolf Valentino was the first male star to be sold on sex appeal. The studio publicity reported how women fainted when they saw him. When he died in 1926, over 100,000 fans lined the streets during his funeral.

The release of the first 'talkie' in 1927 made the cinema even more popular. By 1930 more than 100 million cinema tickets were sold every week. Movie-makers found that sex sold tickets. Newspapers wrote about risqué love scenes and the sex lives of the stars.

The cinemas themselves improved their facilities in order to attract more people. The early nickelodeon with its wooden seats was replaced by 'picture palaces' with luxurious seats. The hollow-sounding piano was replaced by organs or even a full orchestra. By the end of the 1920s, there were several famous film studios, notably Warner Brothers, William Fox and Metro-Goldwyn-Mayer (MGM).

Source C: Mary Evelyn Hults remembers the 1920s

It was really an experience. You would be treated like a king or queen. You were ushered into an enormous lobby of marble or gilt with huge stairways leading up to the balconies. All the carpets were at least an inch or two thick. Everything was done in there to make you feel comfortable, to make you feel very important.

THE RADIO

The radio had a huge influence on many Americans. The first radio station, Station KDKA, began in 1920, and by 1930, 40 per cent of US homes had a radio set. Radio enabled people to listen to sporting events, music – notably jazz – and advertisements. News, sport and entertainment were easily relayed into millions of homes. Indeed radio became the main source of family entertainment. It created sporting heroes such as Jack Dempsey and Babe Ruth, and made events accessible to many who could not afford to attend.

Source B: A woman listening to a radio, 1923

Tasks

1. *Make a mind map of the main forms of entertainment. On your mind map show any links. For example, the radio could be used to promote sport.*

2. *Study Sources A and B. How important was the media in promoting new forms of entertainment?*

3. *What can you learn from Source C about why the cinema became popular?*

4. *Explain how two forms of entertainment became popular in the 1920s. (For guidance on how to answer this type of question, see page 93.)*

Hollywood

Hollywood became the centre of movie making in the USA in the 1920s.

The first film shot in the Hollywood area was called *In Old California* (1910). The following year the first studio was opened by the Centaur Company. This company was based in New Jersey but wanted to make Western films in California. By 1915 the majority of American films were being made in the Los Angeles area. Four major film companies – Paramount, Warner Bros, RKO and Columbia – had studios in Hollywood. Five years later, a million people were employed in the Hollywood film industry.

Movie stars themselves moved to the Los Angeles area and began building themselves luxury homes. Gloria Swanson, for example, had a 22-room mansion in Beverly Hills. Charlie Chaplin and Buster Keaton both lived in the area.

Hollywood and the film industry in general did provoke criticism from those who believed that the movies were threatening the morals of American society. Many Americans blamed Hollywood for the blatant use of sex symbols, such as Clara Bow and Rudolf Valentino. They were also shocked by the morality of some Hollywood films. Hollywood responded by setting up the Hays Code.

Source A: Extracts from the Hays Code

- *No screen nudity*
- *Screen kisses must not last*
- *Adultery must not be presented as attractive*
- *Producers must avoid low, disgusting, unpleasant, though not necessarily evil, subjects*
- *Members of the clergy cannot be comic characters or villains*
- *Murder, arson and smuggling must be shown as evil.*

Tasks

5. *What can you learn from Source A about attitudes to film making in the 1920s?*

6. *Source B was used to advertise the film* The Kid. *Devise an appropriate caption to encourage people to go to see the film.*

Biography Charlie Chaplin, 1889–1977

Charlie Chaplin was born in England in 1889 and moved to the USA in 1913. He began to work in silent movies and rose to become one of the great comic movie stars of the 1920s. Among his most famous films were *The Vagabond*, *The Kid*, *The Gold Rush* and *The Pawnshop*.

Source B: Charlie Chaplin and Jackie Coogan in *The Kid*, 1921

Chaplin did lose popularity in the 1920s when an actress, Joan Barry, claimed he was the father of her child. Chaplin took Barry to court over this. Although he won the case, some Americans turned against him, believing he was setting a bad moral example, and refused to go to see his films.

What was meant by the 'jazz age'?

The 1920s is known as the 'jazz age' because the popular music of the time was jazz. The writer F Scott Fitzgerald coined the phrase in 1922 in his book *The Beautiful and Damned*.

Jazz was not new. It originated with black slaves who were encouraged to sing in order to increase production. They used washboards, cans, pickaxes and percussion to produce their own distinctive brand of music. By changing the beat and creating particular rhythms, it was changed into jazz. Originally the music had various names, including 'blues', 'rag' and 'boogie-woogie'. However, these words were taken from black sexual slang terms, and white people disapproved of their use. Therefore, the music was renamed jazz.

Despite its African American origins, in the 1920s jazz became popular with young middle-class whites, especially the flappers. Some condemned jazz as another sign of a fall in moral standards. In 1921, for example, the *Ladies Home Journal* published an article with the title 'Does Jazz put the Sin in Syncopation?' (Syncopation refers to the off-beat rhythms that characterise jazz music.)

Some cities, including New York and Cleveland, prohibited the public performance of jazz in dance halls. However, this only made it more exciting to the young. Jazz became the great attraction of the night clubs and speakeasies and was brought into homes through radio broadcasts.

Duke Ellington, 1899–1974	Louis Armstrong, 1901–1971

He was born in Washington, DC, in 1899 and became a composer and pianist. In the 1920s he moved to New York, where he assembled a ten-piece band. He became popular because of recordings such as *Choo Choo* and *Chocolate Kiddies*.	He was born in New Orleans in 1900 and became famous as a trumpeter there. In 1922 he moved to Chicago, known as the jazz capital of the USA. By 1925 he had his own band and was known nationwide. Some of his famous recordings included *Ain't Misbehavin* and *Tiger Rag*.

Source A: The *Ladies Home Journal*, 1922

Jazz was originally the accompaniment of the voodoo dancer, stimulating the half-crazed barbarian to the vilest deeds. The weird chant had been employed by other barbaric people to stimulate brutality and sensuality. That this has a demoralising effect on the human brain has been demonstrated by many scientists. Jazz is harmful and dangerous and its influences are wholly bad.

Task

What can you learn from Source A about attitudes to jazz in the 1920s?

Examination practice

This section provides guidance on how to answer question 1b from Unit 2, which is worth six marks. There is further guidance on how to answer this type of question on page 31.

Question 1 – describe

Describe the key features of the flapper movement of the 1920s. (6 marks)

How to answer

- Underline key points in the question.
- Plan your answer. Think of the relevant points – the main question word is 'describe', and the topic is the flapper movement. You will need to describe three key features.
- Fully develop each factor/feature you mention. Features could include:
  - How flappers looked
  - Their attitude to socialising
  - F Scott Fitzgerald
  - Attitudes to flappers

The more precise your knowledge, the higher your marks.

- Make links between one factor/feature and the next. Use link words or phrases, such as 'furthermore', 'moreover', 'however', 'in addition', 'as a result of', and 'this led to'.
- Aim for two good length paragraphs, as the question is worth six marks.

The diagram below shows the steps you should take to write a good answer. Use the steps and the examples to complete the answer to the question. Write your answer one paragraph at a time and link the paragraphs where possible.

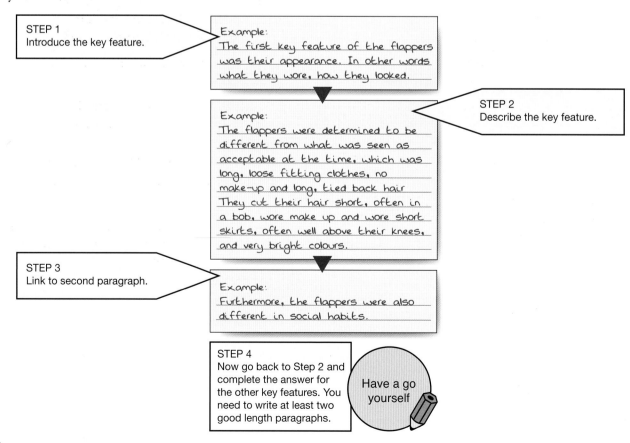

STEP 1
Introduce the key feature.

Example:
The first key feature of the flappers was their appearance. In other words what they wore, how they looked.

STEP 2
Describe the key feature.

Example:
The flappers were determined to be different from what was seen as acceptable at the time, which was long, loose fitting clothes, no make-up and long, tied back hair. They cut their hair short, often in a bob, wore make up and wore short skirts, often well above their knees, and very bright colours.

STEP 3
Link to second paragraph.

Example:
Furthermore, the flappers were also different in social habits.

STEP 4
Now go back to Step 2 and complete the answer for the other key features. You need to write at least two good length paragraphs.

Have a go yourself

Prohibition and gangsters

Source A: A pro-Prohibition cartoon published in 1917

Daddy's in There---

And Our Shoes and Stockings and Clothes and Food Are in There, Too, and They'll Never Come Out.

—*Chicago American.*

Task

What can you learn from Source A about US attitudes to alcohol?

During the nineteenth century, many groups in the USA had supported the idea of prohibiting the sale of alcohol. The Women's Christian Temperance Union (established in 1873) and **Anti-Saloon League** (1895) were very powerful organisations. They made the idea of Prohibition one of the top political issues. Their success is shown by the fact that in the years from 1906 to 1919, 26 American states passed laws to limit the sale of alcohol. The USA was not alone in facing demands for restrictions on alcohol – by 1919 Russia, Iceland, Norway, Finland and parts of Canada had introduced Prohibition. When Prohibition was introduced in the USA it was called the 'noble experiment'. However, it created as many problems as it solved – most notably by spreading gangsterism and organised crime. President Franklin Roosevelt ended Prohibition in 1933.

This chapter answers the following questions:

- Why was Prohibition introduced?
- What effects did Prohibition have on US society?
- What was the importance of gangsters?

Examination skills

This chapter gives guidance on question 1c from Unit 2. This question, which is worth eight marks, is a consequence question.

Why was Prohibition introduced?

Momentum for Prohibition had been building up before the USA entered the First World War in 1917. From that point forward, the Prohibition campaign gathered pace. Female reformers had argued for some time that there were clear links between consumption of alcohol, and wife-beating and child abuse. Henry Ford and other **industrialists** were concerned that drinking reduced efficiency and output at work. Many religious groups saw alcohol as the root of sin and evil and were keen to support Prohibition. It was felt that Prohibition would support and strengthen the traditional values of the American people, who were God-fearing, hard-working, family-oriented and **thrifty**. Moreover, it would encourage immigrants to follow these values.

America's participation in the war created many problems around the issue of Prohibition. Many brewers were of German origin, and when the USA declared war on Germany, the **Temperance Movement** and the Anti-Saloon League saw prohibiting the sale of alcohol as a **patriotic** issue. Their followers viewed the sale and consumption of alcohol as a betrayal of the USA.

As anti-German feeling grew in the USA, beer was given the nickname 'the Kaiser's brew' (the Kaiser was the German emperor).

In September 1918 President Woodrow Wilson banned beer production until the war ended. There was little opposition to this move – there were not even any organised bodies to counter the arguments of the Prohibition lobby. The Prohibition Amendment, which stopped the 'manufacture, sale or transportation of intoxicating liquors' was ratified in **Congress** in January 1919 and was scheduled to come into effect one year later. The amendment did not outlaw buying or drinking alcohol, nor did it define the term 'intoxicating liquors'. In 1920 Congress passed the Volstead Act, which defined 'intoxicating liquors' as anything containing more than 0.5 per cent

alcohol. The Internal Revenue Service (IRS) became responsible for enforcing Prohibition.

> **Source A: Part of a song, written in 1903, called 'When the Prohibs Win the Day'**
>
> *There'll be plenty of food for eating,*
> *There'll be plenty of clothes for wear,*
> *There'll be gladness in ev'ry meeting,*
> *There'll be praise to outmeasure prayer,*
> *There'll be toys each day for baby,*
> *And then Papa at home will stay,*
> *And a heaven on earth will the bright home be,*
> *When the Prohibs win the day.*

> **Source B: From an Anti-Saloon League pamphlet, 1918**
>
> *The American's patriotic duty is to abolish the un-American, pro-German, crime-producing, food-wasting, youth-corrupting, home-wrecking, treasonable liquor traffic.*

> **Source C: A cartoon published in a US newspaper during the First World War**

Tasks

1. *What do Sources A and B show you about the ideas of those who wished to introduce Prohibition?*

2. *What can you learn from Sources C and D about the supporters of Prohibition?*

3. *Design a pro-Prohibition poster showing why Americans should give up alcohol.*

4. *Write a brief attack on Prohibition. (Look back to Chapter 3 for a reminder of its impact of on agriculture.)*

5. *Copy and complete the spider diagram (right) to show why Prohibition was introduced.*

Religious groups saw drinking as sinful

Reasons for the introduction of Prohibition

Patriotism – beer linked with Germany

Chapter 5 Prohibition and gangsters   47

What effects did Prohibition have on US society?

Source A: This 1920s cartoon shows Uncle Sam and a man labelled 'State' arguing, each demanding of the other, 'You do it!' In the background, a smiling 'Bootlegger' stands next to boxes labelled 'Gin', 'Beer', 'Choice Liquor' and 'Handmade Liquor'

Prohibition drove drinkers and drinking underground. It became impossible to prevent people from drinking alochol – and crucially, from drinking beverages with an alcoholic content greater than 0.5 per cent. Huge numbers of people were prepared to break the law not only to produce alcohol but also to go to private bars to consume it. For many ordinary people, consuming alcohol or visiting a 'speakeasy' did not feel like breaking the law. Prohibition created a situation where consumers wanted a product which could not be provided by legitimate means. To satisfy this demand, organised crime stepped in. Thus began the age of the gangster.

The vocabulary of Prohibition

Prohibition developed its own language and vocabulary during the 1920s. The following table shows the most frequently used terms.

Prohibition terms

speakeasy	illegal drinking saloon
bootlegger	one who produced or sold alcohol illegally
bathtub gin	home-brewed gin
still	a device for distilling alcohol
moonshine	illegally distilled or smuggled alcohol
rum runner	someone who illegally transports liquor across a border

Source B: A woman reveals a flask of alcohol hidden in her garter, 1926

Task

1. *What can you learn from Sources A and B about Prohibition?*

Smuggling

It was never difficult to get hold of alcohol. There were many people who produced it illegally and many who smuggled it from Europe, Mexico, Canada and the Caribbean. The USA had more than 30,000 kilometres of coastal and land borders to guard, and so it was extremely difficult to prevent smuggling. It was even possible to find doctors who would prescribe 'medicinal whiskey'.

Speakeasies

Within a short time after the introduction of Prohibition, there were more speakeasies than there had been legal saloons in the old days. In New York alone there were more than 30,000 speakeasies by 1930. An owner of a speakeasy had many overheads. As well as purchasing the illegal alcohol, he would have to pay off federal agents, senior police officers and city officials (and also the police on the beat when deliveries were made). This situation was replicated across the USA.

Health

Prohibition had mixed consequences for the health of Americans. Deaths from alcoholism had fallen by 80 per cent by 1921, but by 1926 about 50,000 people had died from poisoned alcohol. Male deaths from cirrhosis of the liver fell from 29.5 per 100,000 in 1911 to 10.7 per 100,000 in 1929, yet doctors reported an increase in cases of blindness and paralysis – again, as a result of drinking poisoned alcohol.

Many pointed out that Prohibition reduced the number of people killed on the roads, and the incidence of drink-related accidents at work did diminish. Moreover, per capita consumption of alcohol fell during Prohibition.

The brewing industry

Prohibition had a lasting effect on the nation's brewing industry. St. Louis had 22 breweries before Prohibition. Only nine re-opened after Prohibition ended in 1933. The Anheuser-Busch company survived only because it diversified into soft drinks, developed a bottling industry and even manufactured car and lorry parts. In 1915 there were 1,345 breweries in the USA. In 1934 there were only 756.

The end of Prohibition

By the early 1930s, there was clear and growing opposition to Prohibition. However, since the Volstead Act, attention had focused on the moral dimension of the drinking culture. Just as women had attacked the sale of alcohol before Prohibition, they now formed groups to highlight the new alcohol-related problems Prohibition had created.

Many felt that if Prohibition were removed, the legal brewing industry would create jobs. People would pay more in taxes and duties, thus helping to combat the **Depression** in the USA. Franklin Roosevelt called for the end of Prohibition in his presidential campaign. On becoming president, he carried out his promise in December 1933.

> Source C: **Pauline Sabin, founder of the Women's Organization for National Prohibition Reform, speaking in 1929**
>
> *In pre-prohibition days, mothers had little fear in regard to the saloon as far as their children were concerned. A saloon-keeper's license was revoked if he was caught selling liquor to minors. Today in any speakeasy in the United States you can find boys and girls in their teens drinking liquor and this situation has become so acute that the mothers of the country feel something must be done to protect their children.*

Tasks

2. Why was it difficult to prevent the smuggling of alcohol into the USA?

3. What is meant by the term 'speakeasy'? Try to find out the origin of the term.

4. Construct a text message from a smuggler to a speakeasy owner about Prohibition.

5. Design a poster showing how Prohibition helped to create unemployment in the USA.

6. Explain the effects of Prohibition on the people of the USA. (For further guidance on how to answer this type of question, see page 52.)

7. What can you learn from Source C about those who grew to hate Prohibition?

What was the importance of gangsters?

Enforcing Prohibition proved impossible. The Internal Revenue Service (IRS) never had more than 2,500 agents, and some of them became paid hands of the gang leaders. The most famous of the IRS agents was Eliot Ness, the man who eventually arrested Capone.

Most Americans were prepared to break the Prohibition law, and so a new criminal age began. Making and selling alcohol brought huge profits. Police and city officials were aware of the spread of speakeasies and bootleggers, but the lawbreakers realised that bribery would buy silence. One New York politician said it would take 250,000 federal agents to enforce Prohibition and that hundreds more would be needed to check the police. What followed in the 1920s was public corruption on a scale never before seen in the USA.

> **Source A: A cartoon showing Uncle Sam exhausted by the Devil's flow of bootleg liquor**

Task

1. *Describe the key features of the corruption in cities during Prohibition. (Remember how to answer this type of question? For further guidance, see page 44.)*

Al Capone

Biography Al Capone, 1899–1947

1899	Born in New York
1917	Joins the Five Points Gang led by Johnny Torrio
1921	Moves to Chicago to work with Torrio
1922	Becomes a partner in Torrio's saloons, gambling houses, and brothels
1925	Takes over operations when Torrio leaves Chicago
1929	Is responsible for the St Valentine's Day Massacre
1931	Is indicted for income tax evasion and found guilty as charged
1939	Wins release from prison
1947	Dies in Palm Island, Florida

Al Capone epitomises the gangsters of the Prohibition era. The son of Italian immigrants, he left school at an early age and became involved in small-time criminal activities. Capone was given the nickname 'Scarface' following a fight that broke out when he was working as a bouncer at a New York club. His links to the crook Johnny Torrio led him to Chicago, where he eventually rose through the ranks to take over Torrio's operations. Capone cemented his position as one of the leading gangsters in Chicago by bribing local officials. Before long, he had half of the city's employees on his payroll.

Capone controlled the mayor and senior police officers and fixed local elections. In Chicago he controlled speakeasies, bookmakers' joints, gambling houses, brothels, horse and race tracks, nightclubs, distilleries and breweries.

Despite his criminal activities, Capone was seen by many Americans as a glamorous person. He moved in the highest social circles and 'put Chicago on the map'. He was the first person to open soup kitchens after the 1929 **Wall Street** Crash, and he ordered stores to give clothes and food to the needy at his own expense.

In his quest for overall control of all Chicago gangs, Capone was involved in the infamous St Valentine's Day Massacre. He organised the shooting of several leaders of a rival gang, led by Bugs Moran, in broad daylight. It was this incident which made many Americans finally realise that the gangsters, and Capone in particular, were not the glamorous characters they had imagined.

In 1931 Capone was prosecuted for income tax evasion for the years 1925–29. It was claimed that he owed more than $200,000 in taxes from gambling profits. He was subsequently found guilty; his role as gang leader was over. The demise of Capone seemed to herald the end of the age of the gangster. With the Depression setting in, the American people had plenty of other issues to contend with.

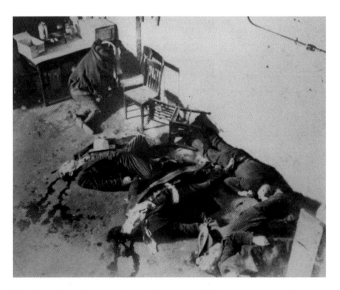

The bodies of gangsters lying on a Chicago garage floor following the St Valentine's Day Massacre, 1929.

Source B: **A poster for the 1932 film** *Scarface*

Tasks

2. *What can you learn from Source A about Prohibition?*

3. *Why did many people consider the gangsters of the Prohibition era glamorous?*

4. *What impression of the USA during Prohibition does Source B present?*

5. *Create your own poster for a film glamorising the gangster age.*

6. *Write an obituary for the Prohibition era.*

Examination practice

This section provides guidance on how to answer question 1c from Unit 2, which is worth eight marks and is the consequence (effects) question.

Question 1 – consequence (effects)

What were the effects of Prohibition on American people? (8 marks)

How to answer

- Underline key points in the question. Doing this will ensure that you focus sharply on what the question wants you to write about.

- Begin each paragraph by stating the effect and then give a fully developed statement about each effect. One developed effect is worth three marks.

- Make links between each effect.

- Aim to write about at least two effects. Two developed and linked effects will achieve the maximum score (eight marks).

The diagram on the right gives you further guidance on how to answer this type of question.

Question 2 – consequence (effects)

What were the effects of the rise of gangsters during Prohibition? (8 marks)

Now have a go yourself

Try answering question 2 using the steps shown for question 1. Remember to:

- write about at least two effects

- fully explain each effect.

STEP 1
State the effect.

Example:
The first effect of Prohibition on American people was that many became prepared to break the law and buy alcohol.

STEP 2
Fully explain the effect.

Example:
The alcohol level in drinks was set at 0.5% and those who were unhappy with this would buy illegal liquor at speakeasies. Some would get hold of it by any possible means and buy directly off the bootleggers – those who manufactured the alcohol illegally. Even doctors prescribed medicinal whiskey. Therefore large numbers of ordinary people had been made criminals by Prohibition.

STEP 3
Try to make links between each of the effects. Remember to use link words or phrases, such as 'furthermore', 'moreover', 'however', 'in addition', 'as a result of' and 'this led to'. This is an example of a possible link between the first change and the second.

Example:
In addition, Prohibition led to large numbers of people manufacturing and distributing alcohol illegally.

STEP 4
Fully explain the effect.

Example:
In some cases this was just ordinary people who brewed their own. In other cases, it was done on a large scale, so that speakeasies could be supplied with huge amounts of alcohol. This production led in turn to the growth of gangsters who controlled production and distribution in cities.

STEP 5
If you can discuss one or two other effects then go back to Step 3.

Have a go yourself

Racism and intolerance

Source A: A report from the *Washington Eagle*, 1921. It describes the death of a black man who had been accused of murdering a white woman in Georgia

*The **negro** was taken to a grove where members of the Ku Klux Klan had placed a fine pine knot around a stump. The negro was chained to the stump and asked if he had anything to say. Castrated and in indescribable pain, the negro asked for a cigarette and blew the smoke in the face of his tormentors. The fire was lit and a hundred men and women, old and young, joined hands and danced around while the negro burned.*

Source B: From the last statement made by Bartolomeo Vanzetti in 1927, just before his execution

I am not only not guilty of these crimes, but I never commit a crime in my life – I have never steal and I have never kill and I have never spilt blood. I would not wish to a dog or a snake what I have had to suffer for things I am not guilty of. I am suffering because I am a radical and indeed I am a radical. I have suffered because I was an Italian, and indeed I am an Italian.

Tasks

1. What can you learn from Source A about the treatment of black Americans in the 1920s?

2. Study Source B. Why does Vanzetti believe he has suffered?

Many Americans benefited from the economic boom of the 1920s. Their standard of living improved, and they enjoyed a wider range of leisure activities and entertainment. However, many people living in the USA were the victims of racism and intolerance. A great deal of intolerance was shown towards foreign-born immigrants, black Americans and those whose beliefs, whether religious or political, seemed to challenge traditional American attitudes. This intolerance resulted in famous court cases, such as the one involving Sacco and Vanzetti, and the 'Monkey' trial. Another significant result of intolerance in 1920s America was the growth of the Ku Klux Klan.

This chapter answers the following questions:

- What was the attitude towards immigrants and immigration?
- What was the 'Red Scare'?
- Why was the Sacco and Vanzetti case important?
- What was the experience of black Americans in the 1920s?
- What was the Ku Klux Klan?
- What was the Monkey Trial?

Examination skills

This chapter provides the opportunity to practise some of the question types from Unit 2.

What was the attitude towards immigrants and immigration?

In the eighteenth and early nineteenth centuries many millions of people **migrated** to the USA from Europe. Most of these immigrants came from Britain, Germany and Scandinavian countries. Many were Protestants and seemed to fit in well with the culture and attitudes of the USA. A new age of immigration began in the second half of the nineteenth century. A large number of Irish Catholics, Italians, Poles, Japanese and Chinese migrated to the US. The number of immigrants reached an all-time high in the years 1901 to 1910.

Tasks

1. *Study Source A. What is the general trend in immigration in this period?*

2. *Study Source B. Can you suggest why so many immigrants are from Western Europe?*

Attitudes to immigrants

The United States prided itself on being a 'melting pot', a place where individuals lost their previous national identity and became Americans. In practice, immigrants found themselves less welcome in the years after 1900 because they provided competition for jobs and brought different customs and attitudes. Some of the reasons for hostility towards immigrants are detailed in this diagram.

Source A: A graph showing the numbers of immigrants arriving in the USA

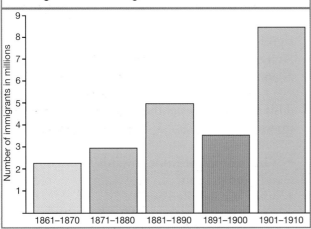

Source B: A graph showing the origin of immigrants arriving in the USA

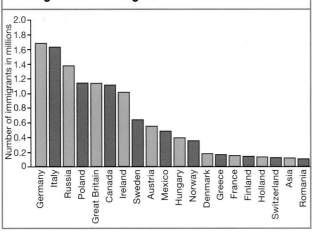

FIRST WORLD WAR

American involvement in the First World War fuelled anti-German feelings and encouraged support for restrictions on immigration. For example, the German language was banned in schools in several states.

ISOLATIONISM

Most Americans did not want to be dragged into another major war. They blamed the First World War on rivalries between countries in Europe and wanted the USA to isolate itself from events in Europe. This included restrictions on immigration from these European countries.

THE 'RED SCARE'

Many Americans feared that immigrants would bring with them dangerous political beliefs, especially communism (see page 57).

Source C: From a speech by a senator from Alabama, 1921

The steamship companies haul them over to America, and as soon as they step off the decks of their ships the problem of the steamship companies is settled, but our problem has begun – Bolshevism, red anarchy, black-handers, kidnappers, challenging the authority and integrity of the flag. Thousands come here who never take the oath to our Constitution and to become citizens of the USA. They pay allegiance to our country while they live upon the substance of their own. They fill places that belong to the loyal wage-earning citizens of America. They are of no service whatever to our people. They are a menace and a danger to us every day.

Source D: A cartoon of 1891. As hordes of undesirable European immigrants arrive in New York City, a judge is telling Uncle Sam (who represents America), 'If immigration was properly restricted, you would no longer be troubled with anarchy, **socialism**, the Mafia and such kindred evils!'

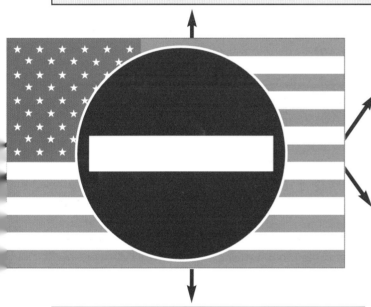

WASPS

For many Americans in the 1920s, the ideal citizen was a 'WASP'– white, Anglo-Saxon, and Protestant. Asian immigrants were not white, and many recent European immigrants were Catholic, Greek Orthodox or Jewish.

QUALITY OF IMMIGRANTS

Many of the new immigrants were poor labourers with little formal education. **Ghettos** began to spring up in the big northern cities. They were often dangerous places riven with drunkenness and violence. Many Americans believed that the immigrants were to blame for these problems.

EMPLOYMENT ISSUES

By 1900 there was not much land available and, as industry became mechanised, the need for workers declined. In addition, many Americans believed that the quality of the immigrants was declining. In the larger cities the more established immigrant groups such as Irish and German Americans tended to look down on the more recent immigrants from Eastern Europe.

Tasks

3. *What can you learn from Source C about attitudes to immigrants?*

4. *Study Source D. What is the message of this cartoon?*

Changes in immigration policy

Immigration was restricted by a series of measures, as detailed in the table below.

Date	Measure	Key features
1917	Literacy test	All foreigners wishing to enter the USA had to take a literacy test. They had to prove that they could read a short passage in English. Many people from poorer countries, especially in Eastern Europe, could not afford to take English lessons and failed the test.
1921	Immigration Quota Act	This act introduced a quota system. The number of new immigrants allowed in from a given country was proportional to the number of people from the same country who had been living in the USA in 1910. The figure was set at 3 per cent. So if there had been 100 Italian immigrants in the USA in 1910, then three Italians were allowed in in 1921. This measure reduced the numbers of immigrants from Eastern Europe because relatively few Eastern Europeans had emigrated before 1910.
1924	National Origins Act	The quota was reduced to 2 per cent of the 1890 census. Since there had been a lot more people from northern Europe living in the USA in 1890, people from these countries now made up a greater proportion of the people allowed to enter.
1929	Immigration Act	This act restricted immigration to 150,000 per year. There were to be no Asians at all. Immigrants from northern and western Europe were allocated 85 per cent of places. By 1930 immigration from Japan, China and Eastern Europe had virtually ceased.

Source E: A cartoon of 1924 comments on the immigrant quotas

Tasks

5. *Study Source E. Devise a caption for the cartoon to appeal to those who opposed the restrictions placed on immigration to the USA.*

6. *Use a mind map to prioritise the various reasons the USA had for restricting immigration. Place the most important reason at 12 o'clock and the other reasons in a clockwise direction in order of importance.*

7. *Working in pairs, using the evidence on pages 53–55 and Sources A-E, prepare arguments for and against setting up immigration controls.*

What was the 'Red Scare'?

The 'Red Scare' was an almost hysterical reaction from many US citizens to developments in Europe in the years 1917–19. It refers in particular to a widespread fear of **communists**.

In Russia in 1917, the **Bolshevik** Revolution led to the establishment of a communist government. In Germany a group of communists known as the Spartacists attempted to seize power in January 1919. Many Americans were convinced that similar dangerous revolutionary ideas were being brought to America by immigrants, especially people from Eastern Europe. Moreover, Americans tended to see any new political ideas, especially radicalism (the belief in extreme change) and **anarchism** as branches of communism. All people who believed in these ideas were classified as 'Reds' (communists).

American fears were heightened by a series of events that occurred in the years immediately following the First World War.

Strikes

There were a great number of workers' strikes in 1919. In all, some 400,000 American workers went on strike. These strikes were protests against poor working conditions and low pay. However, to many members of the American public, the strikes seemed to herald the beginnings of a communist revolution. A **general strike** in Seattle was led by an organisation known as the Industrial Workers of the World (IWW), a name that many found strongly suggestive of communist ideals.

The strikes were often surrounded by violence, either as a result of clashes with the police or when employers used heavy-handed tactics against their striking workers.

Bomb outrages

In the same year there was a series of bombings by extreme anarchist groups. In one famous attack, the home of Mitchell Palmer, the **attorney general** (the head of the US Department of Justice), was

bombed. In April 1919, a bomb planted in a church in Milwaukee killed ten people. In May bombs were posted to 36 well-known Americans.

> **Source A: An anarchist pamphlet called *The Plain Truth*, found near the house of Mitchell Palmer**
>
> *There will have to be bloodshed. We will not dodge. There will have to be a murder. We will kill. There will have to be destruction. We will destroy. We are ready to do anything to suppress the **capitalist** system.*

The press whipped up public outrage and insisted that these bombings were further evidence of a widespread communist takeover plot. The police attacked socialist parades on May Day and raided the offices of socialist organisations. Many innocent people were arrested because of their supposed dangerous political beliefs. Among those arrested were **trade unionists**, black people, Jews and Catholics. The arrests were known as the 'Palmer raids' as they were organised by Mitchell Palmer. In all, between 4000 and 6000 suspected communists were arrested in 36 cities across the United States.

Tasks

1. *What can you learn from Source A about anarchist views?*

2. *Put together a series of newspaper headlines for 1919 about the strikes and bombings. Try to whip up anti-communist feeling. Here is one example of a headline from the time:*

REDS PLANNED MAY DAY MURDERS

Why was the Sacco and Vanzetti case important?

On 5 May 1920, two Italian labourers, Nicola Sacco and Bartolomeo Vanzetti, were arrested and charged with the murder of Fred Parmenter. Parmenter was the paymaster of a factory in South Braintree, Massachusetts. Parmenter and a security guard had been shot by two armed robbers on 15 April. Both men died, but not before Parmenter had described his attackers as slim foreigners with olive skins.

The Sacco and Vanzetti trial began in May 1921 and lasted 45 days. Owing to the heavy publicity given to the case, it took several days to find a jury of twelve men who were acceptable to both the prosecution and defence. In all, 875 candidates were called to the court. On 14 July 1921, the jury delivered a guilty verdict. There were demonstrations all over the USA in support of the two condemned men.

Sacco and Vanzetti took their case to appeal in several higher courts, but all attempts failed. The last appeal was in 1927. The two men were executed by electric chair on 24 August 1927.

The evidence against Sacco and Vanzetti

- They were anarchists who hated American **capitalism** and the US system of government.
- Vanzetti had been convicted of armed robbery in 1919.
- 61 eyewitnesses identified the two men as the killers.
- Sacco and Vanzetti were carrying guns on the day they were arrested.
- The two men told lies in their statements to the police.
- Forensic evidence matched the pistol that killed the guard with the one carried by Sacco.
- Vanzetti refused to take the stand at the trial.

Bartolomeo Vanzetti (left) and Nicola Sacco (right).

The evidence in defence of Sacco and Vanzetti

- Vanzetti refused to take the stand because he feared that his political activities would become a major focus and that he would be found guilty of these rather than the robbery.
- 107 people confirmed the two men's alibi (their claim that they were somewhere else when the robbery was committed). However, many of these witnesses were recently arrived Italian immigrants whose English was poor.
- Some believe that the forensic evidence about Sacco's gun was rigged.
- Evidence from the 61 prosecution witnesses often disagreed in important details. Some witnesses had changed their stories by the time the trial started.
- The two men said they lied to the police because they feared that they would be discriminated against because of their support for anarchism.
- Several other men confessed to the crime.
- The judge, Webster Thayer, seemed determined to find the two men guilty.

Source A: From a statement by a leading American lawyer about Judge Thayer

I have known Judge Thayer all my life. I say that he is a narrow-minded man; he is an unintelligent man; he is full of prejudice; he is carried away by fear of Reds, which has captured about ninety per cent of the American people.

Source B: Demonstrators in Boston in 1925 in support of Sacco and Vanzetti

Source C: Freda Kirchwey was in Germany during the last few weeks before Bartolomeo Vanzetti and Nicola Sacco were executed. She wrote about her reaction to the execution in *The Nation* (28 August 1927)

We've hardly talked about it – but every time we got within range of a newspaper we've rushed to it hoping, without any real hope, that some miracle of mercy would have descended on the Governor or someone else. It was hard to sleep through some of those nights. And everywhere we went – from Paris and Berlin to Heiligenblut in the Austrian Tyrol – people talked to us about it with horror and a complete inability to understand. It whipped up further opposition to immigrants, intensified the 'Red Scare' and seemed to strengthen the case for restrictions on immigration.

Source D: Proclamation from the governor of Massachusetts, August 1977

Therefore I, Michael S Dukakis, hereby proclaim Tuesday, August 23, 1977, Nicola Sacco and Bartolomeo Vanzetti Memorial Day and declare, further, that any stigma and disgrace should be forever removed from the names of the two men.

Importance of the trial

- The trial was reported all over the world and showed the intolerance of US society. As Italian immigrants, the two men were victims of racial **discrimination** and were denied rights they were entitled to.

- It exposed the unfairness of the American legal system. The two men were convicted on flimsy evidence, although subsequent evidence suggested that Sacco may have been guilty.

- In the 1970s the Governor of Massachusetts granted Sacco and Vanzetti a formal pardon and agreed that a mis-trial had taken place.

Tasks

1. *Do sources A and D prove that the men were innocent? Explain your answer.*

2. *Examine the evidence for and against the two men, then copy and complete the following grid.*

	Guilty	Not guilty
Most convincing evidence		
Least convincing evidence		

3. *Now make your own decision: guilty or not guilty? Write a paragraph explaining your decision.*

What was the experience of black Americans in the 1920s?

Source A: **A segregated drinking fountain**

FOR COLORED ONLY

Source B: **From an article published in a newspaper for black Americans, 1921**

Look around at your cabin, look at the dirt floor and the windows without glass! Then ask your folks already up North about the bathrooms with hot and cold water . . . What chance has the average black man to get these down home? And if he does get them, how can he be sure but that some night some poor white man will get his gang together and come round and drive him out?

The majority of black Americans did not benefit from the economic boom of the 1920s. They were still seen as second-class citizens. Especially in the South, blacks were **segregated** and suffered from discrimination and often terrible intimidation.

The Jim Crow laws

Africans had been brought to America as slaves in the seventeenth and eighteenth centuries. By the time slavery was ended in the 1860s, there were more black people than whites living in the American South. After the Civil War ended in 1865, 41 state governments, fearing the growing power of black Americans, introduced laws to control black people's freedom. They were known as the Jim Crow laws after a song of 1830. The song, which portrayed black people as childlike and inferior, featured a song-and-dance caricature of black Americans.

Under the Jim Crow laws, the state governments segregated blacks from whites in schools, parks, hospitals, swimming pools, libraries and other public places. After the First World War, new Jim Crow laws in some states extended segregation to taxis, race tracks and boxing matches.

Black Americans found it hard to get fair treatment. They could not vote and were denied access to good jobs and a reasonable education. They were intimidated by whites, who tried to control them through fear. In total, 360,000 black Americans served in the First World War, but they returned home to find that racism was still part of everyday life. In 1919 at least 70 black people were lynched in the southern states. Generally speaking, police there turned a blind eye.

Migration north

Faced by racism and living in often chronic poverty, thousands of southern black Americans

Tasks

1. *What was meant by segregation against blacks in the southern states? You could use a sketch to show the meaning.*

2. *What can you learn from Source B about the reasons for black migration to the north?*

moved to the cities of the north in the years after 1910, hoping to find a better life. The black population of Chicago and New York doubled in the 1920s: Chicago from 110,000 to 230,000, and New York from 150,000 to 333,000.

However, conditions in the North were not much better. Blacks were given poorly paid jobs and were the first to be laid off in bad times. They generally lived in squalid tenement ghettos and faced even more racial intolerance. For example, in Chicago in 1919, gangs of Irish and Polish immigrants attacked blacks who tried to use public facilities. In New York and Chicago they often lived in worse housing than whites yet paid higher rents. They had inferior education and health services.

Improvements

There were some improvements for black Americans in the years after 1918, especially in the northern states.

- In Chicago and New York there was a growing black middle class. Middle-class blacks used their position to bring about change. For example, they boycotted department stores in Chicago until the stores agreed to employ black assistants.
- Jazz brought fame to several black singers and musicians, such as Louis Armstrong (see page 43).
- The black neighbourhood of Harlem in New York became the centre of the Harlem Renaissance – a flourishing of black singers, musicians, artists, writers and poets.
- Black theatre attracted big audiences. Black performing artists, including singers, comedians and dancers, were popular in clubs and musical shows.
- Life expectancy for blacks increased from 45 in 1900 to 48 in 1930.

Below are some examples of influential black Americans of the 1920s.

Paul Robeson, 1898–1976
Paul Robeson was a trained lawyer who was unable to find work because he was black. Instead, he turned to acting and became well known for his role in the hit musical *Showboat.* He became one of the most popular concert singers of his time with songs such as his trademark 'Ol' Man River'. His *Othello* was the longest-running Shakespeare play in Broadway history. More than any other performer of his time, Robeson believed that famous people have a responsibility to fight for justice and peace.

Countee Cullen, 1903–1946
Countee Cullen had an unusual education which ran against the prejudices of the time. He attended DeWitt Clinton High School, whose students were mainly white males. There, he became vice-president of his class during his senior year. He attended New York University and graduated in 1925. Cullen became a renowned poet whose works were published in various literary magazines. His poems attacked racism and highlighted black poverty. In 1927 he wrote two of his most famous poems – 'Ballad of a Brown Girl' and 'Copper Sun'.

Marcus Garvey, 1887–1940
Marcus Garvey thought that black people should not try to be part of white society. He insisted that they should celebrate their blackness and their African past. In 1914 Garvey set up the Universal Negro Improvement Association (UNIA). By 1920 the UNIA had 2000 members. Garvey wanted to establish close contacts with Africa and asked black Americans to use their skills, education and knowledge to make Africa strong and powerful in the world. However, in 1923 Garvey was put in prison for 'postal fraud', and on his release, he was deported. The UNIA fell apart. Nevertheless, Garvey passed on the idea taken up by the Black Power movement of the 1960s that 'black is beautiful'.

W E B Du Bois, 1868–1963
William Du Bois set up the National Association for the Advancement of Colored People (NAACP) in 1910. He wanted America to accept all people and offer equal opportunities to all people. By 1919 the NAACP had 90,000 members in 300 branches. Du Bois used the NAACP to challenge **white supremacy**, especially the segregation laws. He made black Americans much more aware of their civil rights, especially the right to vote. The NAACP also campaigned against the practice of lynching in the South. It investigated and publicised the number of lynchings. Although the NAACP failed to get a law passed banning lynchings, the publicity gained led to a great reduction in the number of lynchings being carried out.

What was the Ku Klux Klan?

Origins

The Ku Klux Klan (KKK) was set up in the 1860s by soldiers who had fought in the American Civil War. Its aim was to terrorise black people newly freed from slavery. However, it died out in the years after 1870 when a federal grand jury determined that the Klan was a 'terrorist organization'. It was revived after the release in 1915 of a film, *The Birth of a Nation*, which was set in the South after the Civil War and showed the Klan saving white families from gangs of blacks intent on raping and looting. The film attracted huge audiences and seemed to reinforce the idea of white supremacy. After the First World War, labour tensions rose as veterans tried to re-enter the work force. In reaction to these new groups of immigrants and migrants, the membership of the Klan increased.

Beliefs

Klansmen were WASPS. They were fighting for 'native, white, Protestant supremacy'. They were anti-communist, anti-black, anti-Jew, anti-Catholic and against all foreigners.

Source A: Hiram Wesley Evans, the leader of the KKK, speaking in 1924

It is the way of the world that each race must fight for its life, must conquer or accept slavery or die. The Klan wants every state to make sex between a white and black person a crime. Protestants must be supreme. Rome shall not rule America. The Roman Catholic Church is un-American and usually anti-American.

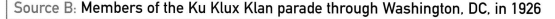

Source B: Members of the Ku Klux Klan parade through Washington, DC, in 1926

Organisation

Klansmen dressed in white sheets and wore white hoods. This outfit was designed to conceal the identity of Klan members, who often attacked their victims at night. The white colour symbolised white supremacy. Members carried American flags and lit burning crosses at their night-time meetings. Their leader, a dentist called Hiram Wesley Evans, was known as the Imperial Wizard. Officers of the Klan were known as Klaliffs, Kluds or Klabees.

Membership

In 1920 the Klan had 100,000 members. By 1925 it claimed to have over five million. It attracted members all over the USA, but especially in the South. Most members were white, Protestant and racist. The state governors of Oregon and Oklahoma were members of the Klan. The second Klan arose in response to:

- Industrialisation, which brought more and more workers to cities. The Klan grew rapidly in cities such as Memphis and Atlanta, which expanded quickly after 1910.
- Many of these workers were immigrants from eastern and southern Europe, or black Americans migrating from the southern states to the urban centres of the North.
- Southern whites resented the arming of black soldiers during the First World War.

Activities

Members of the Klan carried out lynchings of black people and beat up and mutilated anyone they considered to be their enemy. They stripped some of their victims and put tar and feathers on their bodies. For example, in 1921 Chris Lochan, a restaurant owner in Louisiana, was run out of town because he was accused of being a foreigner. His parents were Greek.

Source C: A description of Klan activities in Alabama in 1929

A lad whipped with branches until his back was ribboned flesh . . . a white girl, divorcee, beaten into unconsciousness in her home; a naturalised foreigner flogged until his back was a pulp because he married an American woman; a negro lashed until he sold his land to a white man for a fraction of its value.

Source D: A report of KKK activities by the New York magazine *World* in 1921

5 kidnappings	*41 floggings*
43 orders to negroes to leave town	*1 branding with acid*
	1 mutilation
27 tar-and-featherings	*4 murders*

Decline

The Klan declined after 1925 when one of its leaders, Grand Wizard David Stephenson, was convicted of a sexually motivated murder. When the Governor of Indiana refused to pardon him, Stevenson produced evidence of illegal Klan activities. This event discredited the Klan and led to a decline in membership.

Tasks

1. *What can you learn from Source A about the aims of the KKK?*

2. *Why do you think KKK members wore hoods?*

3. *Using Sources B, C and D draw a poster to campaign against the activities of the KKK. The poster's aim should be to shock people.*

What was the Monkey Trial?

The Monkey Trial was a famous trial that exposed the great differences between the beliefs held by rural and urban Americans.

Background

Most people living in the towns and cities of the USA accepted Charles Darwin's theory of evolution. According to Darwin's theory, modern humans had evolved from ape-like creatures over a period of millions of years. However, this theory was not accepted by many living in rural areas – especially those in the so-called '**Bible Belt**' states, such as Tennessee. Many people living in these areas held very strong Christian beliefs. Known as Fundamentalists, they believed, for example, that the biblical account of the origin of the world – in which God created humans on the sixth day – was literally true.

Source A: A sermon by Billy Sunday, a well-known Fundamentalist, 1925

If anyone wants to teach that God-forsaken hell-born, bastard theory of evolution, then let him… but do not expect the Christian people of this country to pay for the teaching of a rotten, stinking professor who gets up there and teaches our children to forsake God and makes our schools a clearing-house for their God-forsaken dirty politics.

The dispute

The governments of six US states, led by William Jennings Bryan, a leading member of the **Democratic Party**, decided to ban the teaching of Darwin's theory of evolution in their schools. A biology teacher called John Scopes decided to challenge this ban. He deliberately taught evolution in his class in Tennessee in order to be arrested and put on trial.

The trial

Scopes got his trial, and both sides hired the best lawyers. The trial, which took place in July 1925, captured the imagination of the public. Scopes was convicted of breaking the law. However, the trial was a disaster for the public image of the Fundamentalists. Bryan was shown to be confused and ignorant, while the media mocked the beliefs of those who opposed the theory of evolution.

Source B: A report on the trial in the *Baltimore Evening Sun*, July 1925

For nearly two hours Mr Darrow goaded his opponent. He asked Mr Bryan if he really believed that the serpent had always crawled on its belly because it tempted Eve, and if he believed Eve was made from Adam's rib. Bryan's face flushed under Mr Darrow's searching words and when one stumped him he took refuge in his faith and either refused to answer directly or said in effect: 'The Bible states it; it must be true'.

Tasks

1. *What can you learn from Source A about the views held by Fundamentalists in rural America?*

2. *What is the message of Source B?*

Examination practice

Here is an opportunity to practise several of the question types that you will encounter in the exam.

Question 1 – source inference

> **Source A: A historian writing about the Ku Klux Klan in 1992**
>
> *The Ku Klux Klan believed white, Protestant America had to be saved from black people, immigrants, Jews and Catholics. They used extreme violence against people from all these groups, especially black people. Klan members swore an oath of loyalty to the USA and promised to defend the USA against 'any cause, government, people, sect or ruler that is foreign to the country'.*

What does Source A tell us about the Ku Klux Klan? (4 marks)

- For maximum marks you will need to explain at least two supported messages.
- Begin your answer with 'This source suggests...' This should help you get messages from the source.
- For further guidance, see page 26.

Question 2 – describe

Describe the key features of the Monkey Trial of 1925. (6 marks)

- You will need to describe at least three features.
- Remember to fully develop each feature.
- For further guidance, see page 44.

Question 3 – consequence (effects)

Explain the effects of the Red Scare on the USA in the years after the First World War. (8 marks)
- Focus on effects.
- Give at least two effects and fully explain each.
- Make links between each effect.
- For further guidance, see page 52.

Question 4 – causation

Explain why black Americans were often second-class citizens in the USA in the 1920s. (8 marks)
- Focus on reasons.
- Give at least two reasons and fully explain each.
- Make links between each reason.
- For further guidance, see page 74.

Question 5 – change

Explain how attitudes towards immigration changed in the USA in the years after 1929. (8 marks)
- Focus on change.
- Give at least two changes and fully explain each.
- Make links between each reason.
- For further guidance, see page 84.

Question 6 – scaffolding

Was the Sacco and Vanzetti case the worst example of intolerance in the USA in the 1920s?

> You may use the following information to help you with your answer:
> - Sacco and Vanzetti
> - The Monkey Trial
> - Immigration
> - The Ku Klux Klan

(16 marks)

- Focus on answering the actual question rather than just describing the scaffolding points.
- Write one paragraph on at least three of the scaffolding points or three points of your own.
- You can make use of the scaffolding to add an additional point or add a point of your own.
- Make judgements on the importance of each point.
- In your conclusion make an overall judgement which relates to the question.
- For further guidance, see page 119.

Key Topic 3: The USA in Depression 1929–33

Source A: **Unemployed workers at the end of a hunger march from Pittsburgh to Washington, DC, in January 1932**

Task

*What can you learn from Source A about the **Depression** in the USA?*

This key topic examines the causes and consequences of the **Wall Street** Crash. It looks at the weaknesses of the US economy and how the Crash came about. It then examines how President Hoover reacted to the ensuing Depression and the measures he took to strengthen the ailing economy. There is also an analysis of the impact of the Depression on the American people in the years to 1932.

Each chapter explains a key issue and examines important lines of enquiry as outlined below:

Chapter 7 Causes and consequences of the Wall Street Crash (pages 67–74)

- What were the long-term reasons for the Wall Street Crash?
- What were the immediate reasons for the Wall Street Crash?
- What were the effects of the Crash?

Chapter 8 Government reaction 1929–32 (pages 75–84)

- How did President Hoover tackle the Depression and unemployment?

- What were the 'Hoovervilles'?
- How did Hoover deal with the Bonus Marchers?
- What were Hoover's successes and failures?

Chapter 9 The impact of the Depression on people's lives (pages 85–93)

- What were the effects of the Depression on people in the cities of the USA?
- How did the Depression affect people in the countryside?
- What was the 'dust bowl'?

7 Causes and consequences of the Wall Street Crash

Source A: **A stockbroker trying to sell his car the day after the Wall Street Crash, 1929**

$100 WILL BUY THIS CAR MUST HAVE CASH LOST ALL ON THE STOCK MARKET

Task

Look at Source A. Why do you think the stockbroker is trying to sell his car?

In October 1929, the prices of shares on the US **stock market** crashed. This catastrophe was due to long term problems with the US economy, especially overproduction and over-speculation on the stock market. The immediate effects of the Wall Street Crash were disastrous for the USA and many other countries in Europe, especially Britain and Germany. In America, banks literally went bankrupt. The result was economic depression and very high unemployment. The roaring twenties had come to an abrupt and, in many cases, unfortunate end.

This chapter answers the following questions:

- What were the long-term reasons for the Wall Street Crash?
- Why were the immediate reasons for the Wall Street Crash?
- What were the effects of the Crash?

Examination skills

This chapter gives guidance on answering question 1d from Unit 2. This question, which is worth eight marks, is a causation question.

What were the long-term reasons for the Wall Street Crash?

The Wall Street Crash

In the autumn of 1929, the stock market crashed. The fortunes of many Americans were wiped out. The Crash ushered in the Great Depression of the 1930s – the worst economic decline in the history of the USA. It was a time when millions of Americans could not find work, thousands were turned out of their homes, and many roamed the land in railway wagons. Banks failed, and people lost their life savings.

The Great Depression changed the American way of thinking. The government took a more active role in the peace-time economy than ever before. For the first time, it assumed responsibility for relief.

There were several reasons why the Crash happened in 1929, including:

- Overproduction
- Unequal distribution of wealth
- US **tariff** policy
- Over-speculation on the stock market
- Panic selling in 1929.

Overproduction

The problems created by overproduction are shown in the diagram on the right.

Unequal distribution of wealth

The new-found wealth of the 1920s was not shared by everyone. Almost 50 per cent of American families had an income of less than $2000 a year, the minimum needed to survive. They could not afford to buy the new **consumer goods**. Some manufacturers did not see that there was a limit to what could be bought, and so they continued to produce goods. The result was overproduction.

US tariff policy

The USA could not sell its surplus products to other countries, especially in Europe, for two reasons:

- Some European countries owed the USA huge amounts of money and were struggling with repayments.

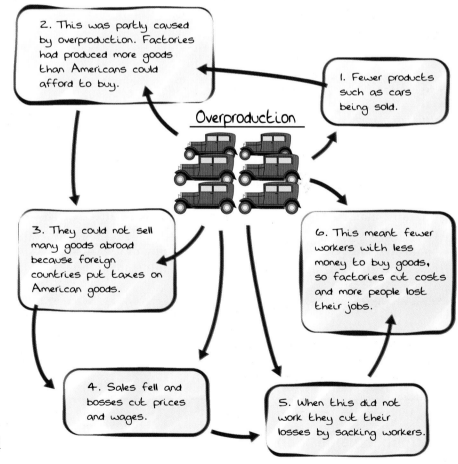

Overproduction

2. This was partly caused by overproduction. Factories had produced more goods than Americans could afford to buy.

1. Fewer products such as cars being sold.

3. They could not sell many goods abroad because foreign countries put taxes on American goods.

6. This meant fewer workers with less money to buy goods, so factories cut costs and more people lost their jobs.

4. Sales fell and bosses cut prices and wages.

5. When this did not work they cut their losses by sacking workers.

• The US government had put high tariffs on foreign goods in the 1920s (see page 13). Many foreign governments responded by doing the same to American goods, and consequently US businessmen found it very difficult to sell their goods abroad. Therefore, an ideal outlet for their overproduction was blocked.

Over-speculation on the stock market

During the 1920s, more and more Americans bought shares on the stock exchange, and prices kept rising. In 1928, however, shares did not rise at the same rate as they had risen in previous years. This was because many companies were not selling as many goods, so their profits fell. Fewer people were willing to buy shares, and there was a drop in confidence in the market. This downturn should have been seen as a warning of worse to come. Yet when share prices began rising again, greed took over, and people began to speculate once more.

Source A: A US economist of the 1920s explaining the fears that some Americans had at that time

Sooner or later, a crash is coming, and it may be terrific, factories will be shut down, men will be thrown out of work and there will be a serious business depression.

Source B: A businessman warns in 1928 about the dangers of over-speculation

The number of inexperienced speculators is being increased by a great many men who have been attracted by newspaper stories. The stories yell of the big, easy profits to be made on the stock exchange. These amateurs have not learnt that markets sometimes panic and that there are large falls in prices. These suckers speculate on tips, on hunches. They buy or sell at the slightest notice.

Source C: A graph showing the changes in the price of shares in the USA in the years 1925–33

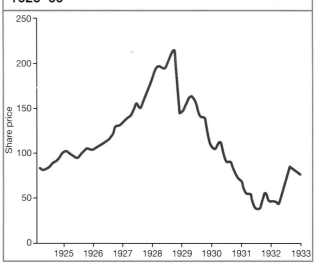

Tasks

1. *Study Source A. Why do you think the economist felt that there would be problems in the future?*

2. *What can you learn from Source C about over-speculation on the stock market?*

3. *Does Source B support the view given in Source C? Explain your answer.*

4. *Draw your own concept map showing all the major reasons for the Wall Street Crash mentioned on these two pages. Add arrows showing the links between the reasons. Using different colours, briefly explain the links in another label, and clearly connect the label to the arrow. An example has been given on the right.*

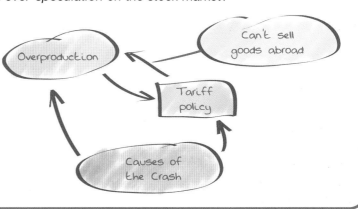

What were the immediate reasons for the Wall Street Crash?

When, in the autumn of 1929, some experts started to sell their shares heavily before their value fell even further, small investors panicked. They saw the fall in prices and rushed to sell their own shares – as can be seen in the bar chart. This led to a complete collapse of prices and thousands of investors lost millions of dollars.

Decline in share values between 1929 and 1932.

The following headlines show the sequence of events that led to the Wall Street Crash.

Wednesday 23 October 1929

More panic in Wall Street

Over two and a half million shares were sold in the last hour of trading today. More and more people are trying to sell their shares and get out of the stock market.

Thursday 24 October 1929

'Black Thursday'

This has been a terrible day on Wall Street. Prices fell so quickly that people have rushed to sell their shares. Nearly thirteen million shares have been traded.

Friday 25 October 1929

Bankers save the day

Bankers met at midday to support the stock market. This ploy seems to have worked, as prices have steadied.

Saturday 26 October 1929

Hoover speaks

President Hoover has assured all Americans that the panic is over and that business and banking will soon recover.

Saturday 19 October 1929

Shareholders begin to panic

Today nearly three and a half million shares were bought and sold. Prices are beginning to fall.

Monday 28 October 1929

Panic returns

Heavy selling again on the stock market. Three million shares were sold in the last hour of business. Dramatic falls in prices.

Monday 21 October 1929

More heavy selling on stock market

Over six million shares bought and sold today. Great fluctuations in prices.

Tuesday 22 October 1929

Stock market recovers

All seems well with prices slightly recovering.

Tuesday 29 October 1929

'Black Tuesday'

The worst ever day on the stock market. Nearly sixteen and a half million shares have been traded. Shares have lost all value. Many shareholders have lost everything. Suicides reported.

Source A: **Traders in Wall Street on Black Thursday, 24 October**

Source B: **Depositors outside a bank in New Jersey, trying to get in to withdraw their deposits on Black Tuesday, 29 October**

Source C: **Cecil Roberts wrote about the Wall Street Crash in *The Bright Twenties*, 1938**

The stock market hysteria reached its peak in 1929. Everyone was playing the market . . . On my last day in New York, I went down to the barber. As he removed the sheet he said softly, 'Buy Standard Gas. I've doubled . . . It's good for another double'. As I walked upstairs, I reflected that if the hysteria had reached the barber level, something must soon happen.

Tasks

1. *What can you learn from Source C about the Wall Street Crash?*
(Remember how to answer this type of question? For further guidance, see page 26.)

2. *Study Sources A and B. Imagine you are a British radio reporter who witnessed these two scenes. Describe to your listeners what you can see.*

3. *Describe the key features of the Wall Street Crash of October 1929.*
(Remember how to answer this type of question? For further guidance, see page 44.)

What were the effects of the Crash?

Unemployment

The impact of the Crash was quite spectacular. By the end of 1929, there were about 2.5 million unemployed in the USA. However, this figure amounted to only 5 per cent of the workforce, and some felt that the country would see out the crisis. However, confidence had died. Those who had money were unwilling to spend.

Unemployment began to gather pace as fewer and fewer consumer goods were purchased – the amount of goods sold in retail stores halved in the years 1929–33. Suddenly the USA became a land of unemployment, tramps, bread queues and soup kitchens. Many people were evicted from their homes and lived on the streets – children included. It was the time of the **hobos** – thousands of men who travelled the country in search of work, hitching rides on railcars and freight wagons.

The Depression

People were not buying goods, and even the rich started to economise. Employers began to lay off employees. Servants were sacked, and those who were able to find jobs worked for less pay than before. The economy was spiralling downwards.

The Depression was not caused by the Crash. To understand what went wrong during the Depression, it is vital to grasp the underlying economic issues of the 1920s – look once more at pages 68–9. However, the Crash did speed up the approach of the Depression, and its effects were catastrophic for the country and the people during the next decade.

- Many stockbrokers were unable to repay their debts to the banks – many banks went bust.
- Thousands of people who had saved money in banks were bankrupted.
- Workforces were laid off.
- There was a collapse of **credit**, and loans were called in.
- Those banks which survived were unwilling to make further loans – the time of speculation and risk-taking was over.

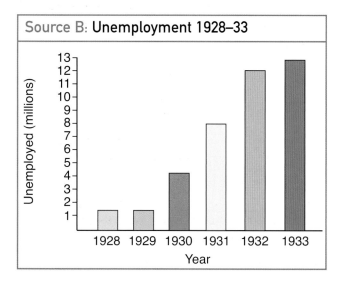

Source B: Unemployment 1928–33

Tasks

1. *What can you learn from Sources A and B about the effects of the Crash?*

2. *Look at Source B. Why would President Hoover have been optimistic about the figures for 1933?*

Farmers were hit terribly, and when they demonstrated in the towns, they carried placards attacking the president. One slogan became extremely popular: 'In Hoover we trusted, now we are busted.'

Source C: **Suicides in the USA**

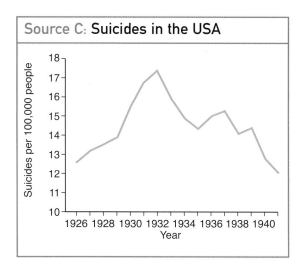

Source F: **Unemployed queuing for cheap food in New York, 1931**

Source D: **From *Toledo: A City the Auto Ran Over*, 1 March 1930, compiled by B Amidon. The writer is looking at the impact of the Depression on a US city**

When I was taken through some of the eighty-seven buildings that make up the plant I was reminded of the old desert towns left in the wake of the gold rush. There was the same sense of suspended life, as I moved among silent, untended machines or walked through departments where hundreds of half-finished automobile bodies gathered dust.

Source E: **From evidence given to Congress in 1931, by the leader of the American Communist Party, about the effects of unemployment on workers in the USA**

Thousands of working class families have been thrown out of their homes because they can no longer pay the rent. In the streets of every large city, workers are dropping and dying from starvation and exposure. Every newspaper reports suicides of these workers who are driven to such desperation.

Tasks

3. *Look at the information and sources on these two pages. Construct a pyramid/triangle to show a chronology of effects – or a fanning/rippling out of effects – so that the reader can see the chain unfold. The top of the pyramid has been done for you below.*

Crash
Panic

Shares sold   Cash-flow problems

4. *Explain the immediate effects of the Wall Street Crash on the USA. (Remember how to answer this type of question? For further guidance, see page 52.)*

Examination practice

This section provides guidance on how to answer question 1d from Unit 2, which is worth eight marks.

Question 1 – causation
Explain why the Wall Street stock market crashed in 1929. (8 marks)

How to answer
- Underline key points in the question – for example, the key theme, dates and the command word.

- Ensure that you focus on causes. Begin each paragraph by stating a cause and then fully develop each cause you give. Use precise knowledge which will impress the examiner, such as specific dates, statistics and names.

- Make links between one cause and the next. Use link words or phrases, such as 'furthermore', 'moreover', 'however', 'in addition', 'as a result of', and 'this led to'.

- Aim to write about at least two causes. Two developed causes will achieve the maximum score (eight marks).

The diagram on the right gives you further guidance on how to answer this type of question.

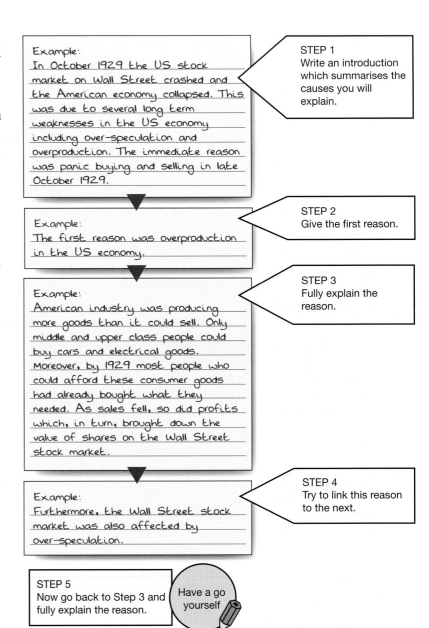

Example:
In October 1929 the US stock market on Wall Street crashed and the American economy collapsed. This was due to several long term weaknesses in the US economy including over-speculation and overproduction. The immediate reason was panic buying and selling in late October 1929.

STEP 1
Write an introduction which summarises the causes you will explain.

Example:
The first reason was overproduction in the US economy.

STEP 2
Give the first reason.

Example:
American industry was producing more goods than it could sell. Only middle and upper class people could buy cars and electrical goods. Moreover, by 1929 most people who could afford these consumer goods had already bought what they needed. As sales fell, so did profits which, in turn, brought down the value of shares on the Wall Street stock market.

STEP 3
Fully explain the reason.

Example:
Furthermore, the Wall Street stock market was also affected by over-speculation.

STEP 4
Try to link this reason to the next.

STEP 5
Now go back to Step 3 and fully explain the reason.

Have a go yourself

8 Government reaction 1929–32

Source A: Part of an article in the *New York Times*, 5 June 1932

Once, the average New Yorker got his shine in an established bootblack parlour paying ten cents, with a nickel tip. But now, in Times Square the sidewalks are lined with new 'shoeshine boys', drawn from almost all walks of life. They charge a nickel and although a nickel tip is welcomed it is not expected. In one block, a recent count showed nineteen shoeshiners. They ranged in age from a sixteen year old, who should have been in school, to a man of more than seventy, who said he had been employed in a fruit store until six months ago. One shoeshine boy said it was more profitable than selling apples – and he's tried them both. According to the Police Department, there are now about 7000 of these 'shoeshine boys' making a living on New York streets. In 1929, they were so rare as to be almost non-existent, and were almost entirely boys under seventeen.

Task

What can you learn from Source A about the impact of the Wall Street Crash?

The impact of the Wall Street Crash and the ensuing Depression in America was quite spectacular. The land of opportunity rapidly became a land of unemployment, tramps, bread queues, soup kitchens and pessimism. For the average citizen, what happened was totally unfathomable. Within a short space of time many Americans found themselves homeless and living at the edge of cities in shacks made of tin and old crates. These places became known as 'Hoovervilles'.

In 1932, after twelve years of government by the **Republican Party**, American voters elected a member of the **Democratic Party**, Franklin D. Roosevelt, president, in the hope that he could pull the USA out of the mire.

This chapter answers the following questions:

• How did President Hoover tackle the Depression and unemployment?
• What were the 'Hoovervilles?
• Who were the Bonus Marchers?
• What were President Hoover's successes and failures?

Examination skills

This chapter gives guidance on answering question 2a from Unit 2. This question, which is worth eight marks, can be one of two types: either a change, or an 'explain how' question. This chapter looks at the change question.

How did President Hoover tackle the Depression and unemployment?

As Secretary for Commerce from 1921 to 1928, Hoover had tried to follow policies that would end the business cycle of boom and bust. In the 1928 presidential campaign, he claimed: 'The USA is nearer to the final triumph over poverty than ever before in the history of any land'. Hoover won the election and was president until March 1933.

Hoover making a speech in 1929. What evidence is there in the photograph to show Hoover's **patriotism**?

Hoover's early policies

Hoover was always optimistic, and his **Quaker** upbringing made him a caring person. For example, he gave his presidential salary to victims of the Depression. However, he has been greatly criticised for allowing the economic situation to worsen after 1930. Nevertheless, Hoover acted quite quickly as the crisis developed and put forward a range of Republican policies to combat the Depression.

Hoover's reaction was to continue to **balance the budget**. He did not wish to borrow money, and his initial actions remained within this framework. He:

- Kept faith with the Republican ideas of *laissez-faire* and '**rugged individualism**'.
- Met business leaders and asked them not to cut wages or production levels.
- Passed the Hawley-Smoot Tariff Act in 1930. This protected US farmers by increasing **import duties** on foreign goods. In retaliation, other countries refused to trade with the USA.
- Encouraged people to give to charities to help the unemployed.
- Suggested that state governments should fund projects to provide new jobs.
- Assisted farmers with the Agricultural Marketing Act of 1930. The act enabled the government to lend money to farmers through special marketing groups. These tried to stabilise prices and sought to ensure that produce was sold at a profit.
- Set up several **relief agencies**, for example the president's Organisation for Unemployment Relief which aimed to promote and co-ordinate local relief efforts. As a result more than 3000 offices were opened.
- Won approval from Congress for $1.8 billion for new construction and repairs to roads, dams, etc. across the USA.
- Cut taxes by $130 million.

Federal v state governments

The USA is a federation or grouping of states with governments which rule themselves and are responsible for local issues such as education. At the centre is an overall **federal government**, represented by the president and **Congress**, responsible for national issues of defence, taxation and foreign policy. Before Roosevelt, the role of the federal government was seen as very limited.

Source A: A collection of statements made by Hoover when president. These statements were part of the Republican Party's ideas

A voluntary deed is infinitely more precious to our national ideal and spirit than a thousand deeds poured from the Treasury.

Each industry should assist its own employees.

Economic wounds must be healed by the producers and consumers themselves.

Each community and each state should assume full responsibility for organisation of employment and relief of distress.

Source B: From a speech by Andrew Mellon, Hoover's Secretary of the Treasury, January 1930, describing the government's optimism after the Crash

I see nothing in the present situation that is either menacing or warrants pessimism. During the winter months there may be some slackness or unemployment, but hardly more than at this season each year. I have every confidence that there will be a revival of activity in the spring and that during the coming year the country will make steady progress.

Source C: From a popular song of the time, called 'I don't want your millions, Mister'

I don't want your Rolls Royce, Mister,
I don't want your pleasure yacht
All I want is food for my babies
Give me my old job back.
We worked to build this country, Mister
While you enjoyed a life of ease
You've stolen all that we built Mister,
Now our children starve and freeze.

Hoover's policies in 1932

However, with unemployment continuing to rise in 1931 and 1932, Hoover had to accept that his policies were not working.

He obtained approval from Congress to establish a relief agency, and the Reconstruction Finance Corporation (RFC) was set up in February 1932, alongside other measures to relieve the crisis (see the following table).

By 1932, the federal government was spending $500 million per year more than it had done in 1928. Despite the interference from Hoover and Congress, the economic situation did not improve and, by 1932, there was increasing opposition to Hoover from many quarters in the USA.

Tasks

1. *What can you learn from Source A about Hoover's ideas on dealing with the economy?*

2. *In what ways does Source B help us to understand the Republicans' reaction to the Crash?*

3. *Copy and complete the table below. Look at Hoover's reactions above. Place each one in the correct column.*

Standard Republican Party policy	Deviation from Republican Party policy

4. *Describe the key features of Hoover's early policies. (Remember how to answer this type of question? For further guidance, see page 44.)*

5. *Study the three measures introduced by Hoover in 1932. What was the purpose of each measure?*

6. *What can you learn from Source C about the impact of the Depression on some Americans?*

What were the 'Hoovervilles'?

Those Americans who lost their homes as a result of becoming unemployed moved to the edges of towns and cities. They built homes of tin, wood and cardboard. These became known as 'Hoovervilles' (an example is shown in the photograph above). There was even a Hooverville in Central Park, New York. Hoover was blamed for the lack of support and relief, and the sarcastic name for the dwellings soon caught on. It has been estimated that at their peak, several hundred thousand people across the USA lived in Hoovervilles.

Hoovervilles had no running water or sewage systems and thus caused health problems for the towns and cities they were in. There were frequent attempts to remove them but there were still Hoovervilles in existence up to 1941, when the government put in a policy to tear them down.

The largest Hooverville was in St Louis, Missouri, where the races were integrated. This did not normally occur. There were also churches and the community even elected its own mayor. In 1936 the Works Progress Administration (see page 108) provided funds for re-locating the workers.

There were other terms using Hoover's name:

- 'Hoover blankets' were layers of newspapers.
- 'Hoover flags' were men's trouser pockets turned inside out to show they had no money.
- 'Hoover leather' was cardboard used to line a shoe with the sole worn through.
- 'Hoover wagons' were cars with horses tied to them because the owners could not afford petrol.

Tasks

1. *Study Source A. Why were Hoovervilles such a source of embarrassment for the Republicans?*

2. *Describe the key features of the Hoovervilles. (Remember how to answer this type of question? For further guidance, see page 44.)*

Who were the Bonus Marchers?

As Hoover gradually became more unpopular, he faced a challenge from an unexpected quarter in 1932. With wages still falling and unemployment still rising, resentment grew. One group, ex-soldiers from the First World War, organised a mass lobbying effort to get aid for themselves and their families.

The government had promised these veterans a bonus for serving in the war, payable in 1945. The veterans felt that they could not wait that long. In May and June 1932, a Bonus Expeditionary Force, made up of over 12,000 unemployed and homeless veterans from all over the USA, marched to Washington, DC, to voice their support of a bill which would allow early payment of the bonuses. They built a Hooverville (called Bonus City) on Anacostia Flats outside the capital and said they would stay there until the bonus bill was passed.

Final estimates put the number of men at 22,000, but with wives and children it is thought there were some 40,000.

Washington, DC, had hardly been affected by the Depression and when the thousands of ragged men and women turned up, government officials labelled them a rabble. This was unjust, because the men organised their Hooverville in a military manner and the protesters were very disciplined.

To pay the bonus would have cost $2.3 billion, and Hoover felt that it was simply too much. Congress supported him. Congress did provide money for transport home for the marchers, but about 5000 refused to leave. Some government officials said that the Bonus Army was led by communists. When the police came in to clear them from some of the old buildings they lived in, conflict broke out and two veterans were killed.

Source A: **Photograph of Bonus Marchers setting up their Hooverville, Bonus City, in Washington, DC, 1932**

Task

1. *Study Source A. Why would a Hooverville in Washington be doubly embarrassing for President Hoover?*

The Battle of Anacostia Field

Photograph of the burning of the Bonus Marchers' Hooverville, July 1932.

Source B: From an interview with A E McIntyre, Federal Trade Commissioner, who witnessed the events of 28 July 1932

When the army appeared, the Bonus people started beating on tin pans and shouted 'here come our buddies'. They expected the army to be in sympathy with them ... The 12th Infantry was in full battle dress. Each had a gas mask and his belt was full of tear gas bombs ... Soon almost everybody disappeared from view, because tear gas bombs exploded ... Flames were coming up, where the soldiers had set fire to the buildings in order to drive these people out.

Source C: US historian F L Allen writing in 1932 about the attack on the Bonus Marchers

Suddenly there was chaos, cavalrymen were riding into the crowd, infantrymen were throwing tear gas bombs. A crowd of spectators was pursued by the cavalry. The troops moved on scattering the marchers and home-going government clerks alike ... that evening the Washington sky glowed with fire.

Hoover responded by calling on the army to control the situation. Orders were sent to Douglas MacArthur, Army Chief of Staff. He was told to disperse the Bonus Marchers. Cavalry units, tanks, infantry with fixed bayonets and a machine-gun detachment marched on the veterans. The camp at Anacostia was razed. More than 100 people were injured, and a baby died of tear gas poisoning in the 'clearance'.

This event became known as the Battle of Anacostia Field, and it left a bitter taste in the mouth of many Americans. It seemed to show the gulf between Hoover and the ordinary American people who were suffering so much as a result of the Depression. Some even thought that the USA was on the verge of revolution.

Task

2. *What do Sources B and C show you about the attack on the Bonus Marchers?*

Source D: From an interview with Studs Terkel in 1970. The interviewee was in the Bonus Army and was describing the attack on the Marchers

On 28 July the great MacArthur came down Pennsylvania Avenue. Behind him were tanks and troops of the regular army. When the Bonus guys wouldn't move, the regular army poked them with bayonets and hit them on the head with rifle butts. The soldiers threw tear gas and vomiting gas . . . They were younger than the marchers. MacArthur was looked upon as a hero.

Source E: From a US newspaper article of the time, about the incident at Anacostia

What a pitiful spectacle is that of the great American government, mightiest in the world, chasing unarmed men, women and children with army tanks.

Tasks

3. In groups of three, make a list of reasons why you think Hoover and Congress were unwilling to pay the marchers. Decide what you think are the most important reasons. Feed back your group's work and put forward your conclusions to the class.

4. Why do you think that Hoover resorted to force against the Bonus Marchers?

5. In groups, role-play a discussion about the reaction to the use of force, with each of you playing one of the following parts:

- *the Bonus Marchers*
- *the soldiers in the regular army*
- *the unemployed*
- *the people of Washington.*

7. How useful are Sources D and E in helping us to understand the events at Anacostia?

Soldiers driving the Bonus Army out of Washington, DC, with tear gas, July 1932.

What were President Hoover's successes and failures?

By 1932, many Americans were demanding action to end the Depression. They were tired of abstract ideals, such as self-reliance and rugged individualism, and talk of prosperity being just around the corner. The ideas of 1928 seemed not to have worked and people wanted change.

Hoover tried various methods but failed to pull the USA out of Depression. His hopes that a prosperous Europe would ease the USA's economic troubles were shattered in 1931, when a financial crisis hit many European countries. He could not escape the fact that the unemployment figures in the USA continued to rise.

However, Hoover did begin to implement policies that were later successfully extended by President Franklin Roosevelt – such as helping banks and home owners. He never, though, fully embraced the ideas that his opponent put forward. Hoover relied too much on the idea of **voluntarism**, and although he did spend federal money, he was unwilling to borrow huge amounts of money.

Congress and many US citizens saw Hoover as a callous and uncaring man. When he said that 'prosperity was just around the corner', those who were unemployed and had no means of support found the comment rather hollow. The riposte of many was: 'In Hoover we trusted, now we are busted'.

When he answered criticisms of his presidency, Hoover was able to point out to his opponents that he had been able to persuade state and local governments to expand their public works programmes and spending by $1.5 billion. Neither Congress nor those involved in business put forward the view that the government should step in to try to solve all of the problems. Hoover did move some towards this philosophy, but he would never have countenanced massive government spending and the creation of huge debts.

Source A: **President Hoover speaking to Congress, December 1929**

I have instituted... systematic... cooperation with business... that wages and therefore earning power shall not be reduced and that a special effort shall be made to expand construction... a very large degree of individual suffering and unemployment has been prevented.

Source B: **A journalist writing at the time of the Bonus March, 1932, describing some of the views that were held about Hoover.**

Never before in this country has a government fallen to so low a place in popular estimation or been so universally an object of cynical contempt. Never before has a president given his name so freely to toilets and offal dumps, or had his face banished from the cinema screen to avoid the hoots and jeers of children.

Source C: **A historian's summary of speeches made by Franklin Roosevelt in 1931. At the time he made these speeches, which describe his views on the role of government, Roosevelt was the Democratic governor of the state of New York**

*When Roosevelt was **governor** of New York, he made it clear that he wanted to help the unfortunate citizens of his state. He said on several occasions that those in office had a moral obligation to help the unfortunate members of society. As the presidential campaign began in 1931, Roosevelt made several speeches which indicated his social responsibility.*

Hoover also pointed out that federal spending on public works during his four-year term exceeded that of the previous thirty years. Some of the most important public works undertaken during this time included the San Francisco Bay Bridge, the Los Angeles Aqueduct, and the Boulder Dam.

Source D: **From a speech by Hoover during the election campaign, 1932**

We might have done nothing. That would have been utter ruin. Instead, we met the situation with proposals to private business and to Congress of the most gigantic programme of economic defence and counterattack ever evolved in the history of the Republic. We put it into action.

The Boulder Dam on the Colorado River under construction in 1933. It was renamed the Hoover Dam in 1947.

Tasks

1. *Study Sources A and D. How did President Hoover show that he had been successful in trying to combat the Depression?*

2. *Study Sources B and C. How did the authors of these sources attack President Hoover?*

3. *Re-read this chapter. What is your verdict on Hoover? Copy the table on the right and complete the balance for Hoover.*

Hoover's successes	Hoover's failures

Examination practice

This section provides guidance on how to answer question 2a from Unit 2, which is worth eight marks. This is the change question. It is similar to the 'explain how' question, which is discussed on page 93.

Question 1 – change

Explain how President Hoover changed his approach to tackling the problems of the Depression in the years 1929–32. (8 marks)

How to answer

- Underline key points in the question: look for the name (President Hoover); the word 'change' and what is changing (Hoover's approach); and the time frame (1929–32).

- Ensure that you focus on change. Begin each paragraph by stating the change and then fully develop each change you give.

- Aim to write about at least two, preferably three changes.

- Make links between one change and the next. Use link words or phrases, such as 'furthermore', 'moreover', 'however', 'in addition', 'as a result of', and 'this led to'.

The diagram on the right gives you further guidance on how to answer this type of question.

Question 2 – change

Explain how the Depression changed the role of the government in the years to 1932. (8 marks)

Now have a go yourself

Try answering question 2 using the steps shown for question 1. Remember to:

- write about at least two changes and preferably three

- fully explain each change

- make links between the changes

STEP 1
State the change.

> Example:
> The first change was that Hoover began to see that some of the Republican policies had to be abandoned.

STEP 2
Fully explain the change.

> Example:
> He wanted to balance the budget but within keeping to that idea, he did begin to interfere more than previous Republican presidents had. The Hawley–Smoot Tariff Act was passed in 1930 with the intention of protecting US industry and the Agricultural Marketing Act of 1930 attempted to protect and assist farmers. More importantly, he asked Congress for money to carry out public works across the USA.

STEP 3
Try to make links between each of the changes (paragraphs). Remember to use link words or phrases, such as 'furthermore', 'moreover', 'however', 'in addition', 'as a result of', and 'this led to'. This is an example of a possible link between the first change and the second.

> Example:
> Moreover, these changes of approach led to Hoover going further in 1932, when his policies led to the government having to borrow money to finance some of the new measures such as the RFC and ERA.

STEP 4
Go back to step 2 and have a go at completing the question by fully explaining the second change, linking it to a third one if you can.

Have a go yourself

9 The impact of the Depression on people's lives

Source A: One of the 'Dust bowl ballads' by Woody Guthrie, written in 1937. Guthrie was a folk singer who **migrated** from Texas to California with the 'Okies' in the 1930s

Lots of folks back East, they say, is leavin' home every day,
Beatin' the hot old dusty way to the California line.
'Cross the desert sands they roll, gettin' out of that old dust bowl,
They think they're goin' to a sugar bowl, but here's what they find
Now, the police at the port of entry say,
'You're number fourteen thousand for today.'

You want to buy you a home or a farm, that can't deal nobody harm,
Or take your vacation by the mountains or sea.
Don't swap your old cow for a car, you better stay right where you are,
Better take this little tip from me.
'Cause I look through the want ads every day
But the headlines on the papers always say:

If you ain't got the do re mi, boys, you ain't got the do re mi,
Why, you better go back to beautiful Texas, Oklahoma, Kansas,
* Georgia, Tennessee.*
California is a garden of Eden, a paradise to live in or see;
But believe it or not, you won't find it so hot
If you ain't got the do re mi.

Task

What can you learn from Source A about the problems faced by people leaving the 'Dust bowl' area?

The impact of the Depression on the people of the USA was in many cases extremely severe. With unemployment reaching 16 million, few people were left untouched. The Depression hit men and women, all races and classes and almost all geographical areas of the USA. Its effects on the American people were profound, painful and long-lasting. As soon as they were able to do so, they voted for change, and in 1932 Franklin Roosevelt was elected president.

This chapter answers the following questions:

• What were the effects of the Depression on people in the cities?
• How did the Depression affect people in the countryside?

Examination skills

This chapter gives further guidance on answering question 2a from Unit 2. This question, which is worth eight marks, can be one of two types: either a change or an 'explain how' question. This chapter looks at the 'explain how' question.

What were the effects of the Depression on people in the cities?

Source A: This re-wording of Psalm 23 was written by E J Sullivan, who had lived in a Hooverville. He called his verse the 1932nd Psalm

Hoover is my shepherd, I am in want,
He maketh me to lie down on park benches,
He leadeth me by still factories,
He restoreth my doubt in the Republican Party.
He guided me in the path of the Unemployed for
  his party's sake,
Yea, though I walk through the alley of soup
  kitchens, I am hungry.
I do not fear evil, for thou art against me;
*Thy Cabinet and thy **Senate**, they do discomfort*
  me;
Thou didst prepare a reduction in my wages;
*In the presence of my **creditors** thou anointed my*
  income with taxes,
So my expenses over-runneth my income.
Surely poverty and hard times will follow me
All the days of the Republican administration.
And I shall dwell in a rented house forever.

Task

1. What can you learn from Source A about attitudes to President Hoover?

Once the crisis began in October 1929, it was not long before factories began to close down. People stopped spending, and as this trend continued, production had to slow down or stop. The industrial cities of the North saw a rapid rise in unemployment. Source A on page 67 clearly demonstrated the impact this situation had on a great many Americans. By 1933 almost one-third of the workforce was unemployed. Once a person became unemployed, it was practically impossible to secure another job.

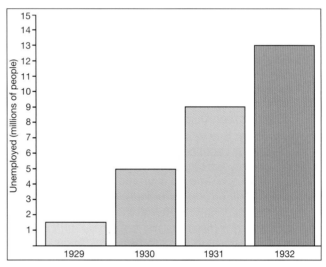

The growth of unemployment. Accurate unemployment figures are not available, because the US government began to record nationwide statistics only in the mid-1930s.

Unemployment

As people lost jobs, they lost their homes. Chapter 8 showed how some built alternative 'homes' in what became known as Hoovervilles. Many of the unemployed in cities simply wandered the streets. They slept in doorways or cardboard boxes or lived in the parks and slept on the benches.

Many men drifted across the USA as hobos. They caught rides on freight trains in search of work. It was estimated that in 1932 there were more than two million hobos. The following year about 6500 hobos were killed – either in accidents or by railroad 'bulls', the brutal guards hired by the railroad companies to make sure the trains carried only paying customers.

Photograph of hobos by a freight train, early 1930s.

Black Americans

When the Depression began, black workers were often the first to be sacked, and their unemployment rate was 50 per cent by 1933. Furthermore, they suffered wage cuts and saw black businesses close down at an alarming rate.

Source B: **From an article 'Negroes out of work', published on 22 April 1931, which examines the impact of the Depression on black Americans**

*The percentage of **Negroes** among the unemployed runs at four, five, six times as their population warrants. When jobs are scarce, preference is given to the white worker in case of a vacancy; but worse than that, a fairly widespread tendency is observed to replace Negro workers with whites. White girls have replaced Negro waiters, hotel workers and elevator operators.*

Source C: **From *Hard Times* by Studs Terkel, 1970. The extract is from an interview with Clifford Burke, a black American who lived through the Depression**

The Negro was born in depression. The Great Depression as you call it didn't mean much to him. The Depression only became official when it hit the white man.

Tasks

2. *What does Source C mean when it says, 'The Depression only became official when it hit the white man?'*

3. *Look at Sources B and C. What do you learn about the position of black Americans at this time?*

Family life

The Depression had a tremendous impact on family life. Marriages fell from 1.23 million in 1929 to 982,000 in 1932. Young people were apparently reluctant to take on this extra commitment when there were few jobs and little prospect of improvements in the economy. There was an accompanying fall in the birth rate. The suicide rate across the USA increased dramatically. From a rate of 12.6 suicides per 100,000 people in 1926, the rate reached a peak of 17.4 (look again at Source C on page 73).

In some states – Arkansas, for example – schools were closed for ten months in the year because there was not enough money to pay teachers. Teachers in Chicago were not paid during the winter of 1932–33. The magazine *Fortune* estimated that in the autumn of 1932 about 25 per cent of the population was receiving no income. Another estimate was that, of the 3.8 million single mothers, only about 20,000 could expect to receive any financial support. In some towns and cities across the USA, where there were not enough soup kitchens and cheap meal centres, people scavenged for food. If there was nothing to scavenge, then they would resort to stealing food.

Because there was no national system of social security, the unemployed and their dependants relied on charitable organisations. Charities such as the Red Cross tried to help, but the scale of the problem was too great. President Hoover established the President's Organisation for Unemployment Relief (POUR), but it simply redistributed money donated by individuals to help people affected by the Depression.

Source D: From *The Lean Years* by H Miflin, 1960, describing the stealing of food by children

By 1932, organised looting of food was a nationwide phenomenon. Helen Hall, a Philadelphia social worker, told a Senate committee that many families with unemployed parents sent their children out to steal from wholesale markets, to snatch milk from babies and to steal clothes to exchange them for food.

Source E: From a speech by Congressman G Huddlestone, 1932. He was addressing a Senate Committee about living conditions in the Depression

Any thought that there has been no starvation is utter nonsense. People are actually starving by the thousands today. They are living such a scrambling, precarious existence, and suffering from lack of clothing, food and nourishment, until they are subject to being swept away at any time, and many are now being swept away.

Tasks

4. *What were the effects of the Depression on family life? (Remember how to answer this type of question? For further guidance, see page 52.)*

5. *Use the information on this page and Sources D and E to write a protest poem about the lack of schooling and food for children in the Depression. Address the poem to the president or the Senate.*

6. *Present an argument for the introduction of a system of social security.*

Photograph of unemployed men at a soup kitchen in Chicago in 1930.

Civil unrest

Many ordinary Americans did not meekly accept the hardships of the Depression. Some of those still in employment went on strike because of the reduced wages they had to accept. Sometimes farmers blockaded roads into towns until they received money for their produce.

Source F: **From an article published in *Time* magazine in October 1931 and written by W Green, a moderate trade union leader**

No social order is secure where wealth flows into the hands of the few away from the many. I warn the people who are exploiting the workers that they can only drive them so far before the workers turn on them and destroy them! The exploiters are taking no account of the history of nations in which governments have been overturned. Revolutions grow out of the depths of hunger.

Source G: **From an interview with Ed Paulsen in 1970. Paulsen had been unemployed in San Francisco during the Hoover presidency**

We'd say 'let's go to City Hall'. There used to be cops on horseback in those days. Sometimes it got to killing. I think on that day three were killed. We were a gentle crowd. We just wanted to go to work ... we weren't talking revolution – we were talking jobs.

Tasks

7. *What does Source G tell us about attitudes to demonstrators at this time? (Remember how to answer this type of question? For further guidance, see page 26.)*

8. *Study Sources D and E on page 88 and then read Source F. Why might some members of the Senate be concerned about the reports given in Sources D and E?*

How did the Depression affect people in the countryside?

Chapter 3 explored the issues US farmers faced during the 1920s. As the Depression took hold, farmers experienced further problems. Bankruptcy among farmers grew because they were unable to sell their produce. In many cases, food was left to rot in the ground. The 1931 drought compounded the farmers' problems when reduced output and falling prices meant that there was no hope of breaking even financially. Between 1930 and 1934 in Nebraska rainfall dropped 27.5 per cent, and as a result, corn crop yields dropped over 75 per cent. The low rainfall continued for much of the 1930s. Crops were damaged not only by the dry weather but also by high temperatures, high winds and attacks from grasshoppers and other insects.

Sometimes farmers would band together to resist – often using force – the re-possession agents who came to take land from those who had not paid their mortgages. For the most part, however, there was little the bankrupt farmer could do other than seek work in the towns and cities, or move to farming areas which were still prosperous.

The dust bowl

The states worst hit by the drought were Texas, Oklahoma, Colorado, New Mexico and Kansas. Poor farming methods had exhausted the soil, and in the drought the soil turned to dust. Therefore, when the winds came, there were dust storms. The affected area, about 20 million hectares, became known as the 'dust bowl' (see Source A). Scientists have estimated that about 850 million tonnes of top soil blew away.

> **Source A: A passage from *From the Crash to the Blitz* by R Cabell-Philips, 1969**
>
> *In the years 1934–38 prolonged drought dried up millions of acres of farmland and pasturage. Dust storms of unprecedented violence darkened the skies from Texas to New York. Floods, hurricanes and tornadoes spread havoc throughout the mid-West. Floods and windstorms during that period killed 3678 and injured 18,791 and damaged more than 500,000 buildings.*

Source B: Farm machinery buried after a dust storm, 1936

Tasks

1. *What does Source A tell us about the impact of the climate on farmers? (Remember how to answer this type of question? For further guidance, see page 26.)*

2. *Write a letter to President Roosevelt explaining why farmers in the Mid-West need government help to combat climate problems.*

The decision to move west

These issues forced more than one million people to leave their homes and seek work in the fruit-growing areas of the west coast. Farmers and their families packed what they could, tied it to their cars and set off for the west. Those from Oklahoma were nicknamed 'Okies' and those from Arkansas were 'Arkies'. The terms quickly became derogatory because the people were seen as threatening. They were suspected of being hobos and possible criminals. Their plight has been captured in Dorothea Lange's photographs (see Sources C and D) and in John Steinbeck's novel *The Grapes of Wrath* (see Source E). Steinbeck's novel and the subsequent film are highly recommended.

Map showing internal migration in the 1930s.

Source C: Migrant mother photographed by Dorothea Lange in 1936 and described by Lange in Source D

Source D: From the memoir of Dorothea Lange, *The Assignment I'll Never Forget*, 1960. Here she is describing meeting one of the migrant workers who has arrived in California – see Source B

I approached the hungry woman . . . She told me she was 32. She said she had been living on frozen vegetables from surrounding fields and birds that her children had killed. She had just sold the tyres from the car to buy food.

Source E: From *The Grapes of Wrath* (1939). The novel was written by John Steinbeck, who won the Pulitzer Prize and the Nobel Prize for Literature

California's a nice country. But she was stole a long time ago. You never will have seen such pretty country. And you'll pass land which is fine and flat with good water supplies and land that's not being used. You go on that land and you plant a little corn and you'll go to jail. You never been called 'Okie'? . . . Well 'Okie' used to mean you were from Oklahoma. Now it means you're a dirty son of a bitch. 'Okie' means you're scum. I hear there's 300,000 of our people there and living like pigs, because everything in California is owned.

Tasks

3. Work in pairs, with one of you presenting a case for moving west and the other a case for remaining. Role-play your discussion in front of the class.

4. Look at Sources C and D. Lange was employed by the government. Does this mean that these two sources are of no use to someone studying the USA in the 1930s?

5. Study Source E, which is from a novel about the 1930s. What limitations does this source have for someone studying the USA in the 1930s?

6. *Explain why farmers decided to move west in the 1930s. (Remember how to answer this type of question? For further guidance, see page 74.)*

Out west

The decision to leave the dust bowl and move west was not taken lightly, for it meant giving up everything. Yet farmers in the west were quite happy to employ 'Okies' and 'Arkies', who would work for very low wages. They would set up camps at the edge of town and seek work wherever they could get it. Naturally, the locals did not like the newcomers – they were taking local jobs – and the police were frequently called in to move the unwanted campers away.

Later, Roosevelt established the Farm Security and Resettlement Administration to tackle these farming issues. Around 650,000 families were given money by the Resettlement Administration, but for many, the intervention was rather late.

An uneven depression

Though unemployment reached 16 million, there were many in the USA who did not experience hardship during the Depression. Most wealthy people remained wealthy, and some were able to buy land and businesses cheaply at the height of the crisis. Personal spending did fall, but as the table opposite indicates, many people had large disposable incomes.

However, the majority of people in the USA did experience problems during the Depression, and 1932 was a presidential election year. The Democratic Party's candidate, Franklin Roosevelt, offered the USA a move away from the Republican approach of minimal interference and rugged individualism.

Two 'Okie' children, from a family of six drought refugees, outside Bakersfield, California, in 1935.

Source G: Personal consumption, 1929–32

Year	Personal consumption ($ billion)
1929	128.1
1930	120.3
1931	116.6
1932	106.0

Source F: From an interview taken by Studs Terkel, an oral historian, in 1970. The interviewee was a psychiatrist in the 1930s

You wouldn't know there was a depression going on ... don't forget that the highest unemployment was less than 20 per cent. My patients paid reasonable fees – I came across a handbook that I had between 1931 and 1934 and in those days I was making $2,000 a month.

Tasks

7. *Explain what is meant by the term 'an uneven depression'.*

8. *How could Hoover use Source F to convince Americans that the economic crisis was not as severe as generally thought?*

9. *How could Roosevelt use Source G to convince Americans that the economic crisis was worsening?*

Examination practice

This section provides guidance on how to answer question 2a from Unit 2, which is worth eight marks. This is the 'explain how' question and is similar to the change question discussed on page 84.

Question 2 – 'explain how'

Explain how the Depression affected people in the cities in the years 1929–32.
(8 marks)

How to answer

- Underline key points in the question: look for the key theme (Depression affecting people in the cities), the command word (explain) and the time frame (1929–32).

- Ensure that you focus on specific points. Begin each paragraph by stating the point and then fully develop each point you mention.

- Aim to write about at least two points.

- Make links between one point and the next. Use link words or phrases, such as 'furthermore', 'moreover', 'however', 'in addition', 'as a result of', and 'this led to'.

The diagram on the right gives you further guidance on how to answer this type of question.

Question 2 – 'explain how'

Explain how farm workers were affected by the Depression in the years 1929–32.
(8 marks)

Now have a go yourself

Try answering question 2 using the steps shown for question 1. Remember to:

- write about at least two points
- make links between each point.

STEP 1
State the point.

Example:
As the Depression deepened, unemployment began to grow with great speed.

STEP 2
Fully explain the point.

Example:
Losing one's job obviously meant that people had no income. It was virtually impossible to secure another job and without money, people had to rely on charity for food. Food queues were a common sight in US cities, as were soup kitchens. Sometimes queues for food stretched hundreds of metres and this led to desperation among the workers.

STEP 3
Try to make links between each of the points (paragraphs). Remember to use link words or phrases, such as 'furthermore', 'moreover', 'however', 'in addition', 'as a result of', and 'this led to'. This is an example of a possible link between the first point and the second.

Example:
Moreover, losing a job frequently led to losing one's home. This led to the building of temporary homes at the edge of the cities – these became known as 'Hoovervilles'.

STEP 4
Fully explain the point.

Example:
They were temporary homes at the edge of the cities named sarcastically after the president. The 'Hoovervilles' were made of card, wood, bits of tin and any scrap materials that could be found. They were a health hazard and most had lots of children living in them.

STEP 5
Now, finish this answer by writing about a third point. This could be about men leaving the cities looking for work – the hobos.

Have a go yourself

Key Topic 4: Roosevelt and the New Deal

Source A: In this 1935 cartoon, the Alphabet Agencies tie down Uncle Sam (the USA)	Source B: President Roosevelt at a Civilian Conservation Camp in Virginia in 1933

Tasks

1. *Study Source A. What is the cartoon's message about the New Deal?*

2. *Does Source B have the same message about the New Deal? Explain your answer.*

This key topic examines the main features of the **New Deal**, including Roosevelt's aims, the 1932 election, the Hundred Days, the **Alphabet Agencies** and the policies designed to deal with agriculture, industry and unemployment as well as the Second New Deal. It also explains the extent and nature of opposition to the New Deal from **Republicans**, some **Democrats**, the **Supreme Court** and popular individuals, such as Huey Long. Finally, it evaluates the successes and failures of the New Deal and the extent of recovery in the years 1933–41.

Each chapter explains a key issue and examines important lines of enquiry as outlined below:

Chapter 10 The nature of the New Deal (pages 95–112)

- Why did Roosevelt win the 1932 presidential election?
- What were the aims of the New Deal?
- What were the 'Hundred Days'?
- What were the Alphabet Agencies?
- What was the Second New Deal?
- What was Roosevelt's role in the recovery?

Chapter 11 Opposition to the New Deal (pages 113–120)

- Why did some individuals oppose the New Deal?
- Why did the Supreme Court oppose the New Deal?
- Why did some politicians oppose the New Deal?

Chapter 12 The extent of recovery (pages 121–125)

- In what ways did the USA recover?
- What were the failures of the New Deal?

10 The nature of the New Deal

Source A: **From President Roosevelt's inaugural speech, March 1933**

This is the time to speak the truth, the whole truth, frankly and boldly. Nor need we shrink from honestly facing conditions in our country today. This great nation will endure as it has endured, will revive and prosper. So first of all let me assert my firm belief that the only thing we have to fear is fear itself. Only a fool will deny the dark realities of the moment . . . This country asks for action and action now!

Task

What can you learn from Source A about Roosevelt's attitude to solving the USA's problems?

Roosevelt won the 1932 presidential election by a landslide. He was very open and honest in his speeches, and he attracted huge numbers of people to his campaign meetings. When he became president, he introduced a series of measures which tackled the **Depression** in a way that was, for the USA, quite revolutionary. For the first time, the **federal government** began to take responsibility for its citizens – the USA had to accept that it would emerge from its troubles only if *laissez-faire* and '**rugged individualism**' were abandoned.

This chapter answers the following questions:

• Why did Roosevelt win the 1932 presidential election?
• What were the aims of the New Deal?
• What were the 'Hundred Days'?
• What was the Second New Deal?
• What was Roosevelt's role in the recovery?

Examination skills
In this chapter you will be given the opportunity to practise some of the question types from Unit 2.

Why did Roosevelt win the 1932 presidential election?

By 1932, many Americans were demanding action. They were tired of ideals like self-reliance and rugged individualism, and talk of prosperity being just around the corner. The ideas of 1928 seemed not to have worked and people wanted change.

Biography   Franklin Delano Roosevelt, 1882–1945

1905	Married Eleanor Roosevelt (a distant cousin of his)
1911–13	Democrat member of New York **state legislature**
1913–20	Assistant Secretary of the navy
1920	Nominated Democratic vice-presidential candidate
1921	Suffered an attack of polio which left him unable to walk properly
1929–33	**Governor** of New York State
1933–45	President of the USA

Though there had been some federal action, there was a growing call for a bolder approach. Such boldness was being shown in New York State by the Democratic governor, Franklin Roosevelt. He had persuaded the state legislature to spend $20 million on helping the unemployed and had introduced old age pensions. Roosevelt had set up a special committee to explore a range of ways to overcome the problems and sought help from all those involved, such as business people, economists and **trade unionists**.

> **Source A: From a speech by Roosevelt in 1931 describing his views on the role of government**
>
> *One of the duties of the government is that of caring for those of its citizens who find themselves the victims of such adverse circumstances as makes them unable to obtain even the necessities for mere existence without the aid of others. That responsibility is recognised by every civilised nation ... To these unfortunate citizens aid must be extended by government, not as a matter of charity, but as a matter of social duty.*

In June 1932, Roosevelt accepted the Democratic Party nomination to run for president. In his acceptance speech he said:

'I pledge you, I pledge myself, to a new deal for the American people.'

Everywhere he went, Roosevelt knew that he had to create a mood of optimism. The despair that many felt was becoming ingrained and he was keen to let people know that he understood their feelings and he would break the cycle of despondency. At meetings, he kept his message simple (as one observer said, 'he always left his vocabulary at home with his dictionary'). He offered a vision and put forward a number of easily understood policies:

- Creation of jobs
- Assistance for unemployed and the poor (relief)
- Government to help both agriculture and industry
- Protection against harsh employers.

Criticisms of Hoover

Were the Republicans responsible for the Depression? While Roosevelt was campaigning to be president, he certainly blamed the Republicans for the USA's dire economic situation. He laid numerous charges at his opponents' door in campaign speeches he gave during 1932. Those charges are described in Sources B and C. Other observers and commentators seemed to share Roosevelt's opinion of the Republican government, as is evident from Source D.

So, was it the failures of the Republican government and Hoover's unpopularity, rather than Roosevelt's solutions for the Depression, that won Roosevelt the election? Some historians have suggested this, as shown in Source E. However, Source F suggests that Roosevelt was prepared to take drastic measures.

Source B: From an election speech by Roosevelt in Iowa, 1932, describing the failings of the Hoover government

I accuse the present Administration of being the greatest spending Administration during peacetime in all our history. It is an Administration that has piled bureau on bureau, commission on commission and has failed to anticipate the needs and the reduced earning power of the people.

Source C: From an election speech by Roosevelt in 1932. He blamed the Republican government for the Depression

First it encouraged speculation and overproduction through its false economic policies. Second, it attempted to minimise the Crash and misled people as to its gravity. Third, it wrongly charged the cause to other nations of the world. And finally, it refused to recognise and correct the evils at home which it had brought forth; it delayed reform, it forgot reform.

Source D: From an election speech by Hoover in 1932. Here he was attacking the policies of Roosevelt

The proposals of our opponents will destroy our system. I especially emphasise that promise to promote 'employment for all surplus labour at all times.' I cannot believe that anyone would be so cruel as to hold out hope so absolutely impossible of realisation to these 10,000,000 who are unemployed. If it were possible to give this employment, it would cost the government $9,000,000,000 a year.

Source E: From *Depression and the New Deal*, by R Smalley, 1990. He is describing the confidence of Roosevelt

Roosevelt showed confidence. The Democratic candidate's smile and optimism proved far more popular with the electorate than Hoover's grim looks. This difference in presentation was important because in some ways the two candidates seemed to have similar policies.

Source F: From an election speech Roosevelt gave in 1932. He is explaining his openness

If starvation and dire need on the part of any of our citizens make necessary the appropriation of additional funds which would keep the budget out of balance, I shall not hesitate to tell the American people the full truth and ask them to authorise the expenditure of that additional amount.

Tasks

1. What can you learn from Source A about Roosevelt's view of the role of government?

2. Why is Roosevelt so critical of Hoover and his administration in Sources B and C?

3. *Describe the key features of Roosevelt's appeal to the American voters. (Remember how to answer this type of question? For further guidance, see page 44.)*

Hoover's defeat

Hoover stayed in Washington for much of the campaign, and when he did make public appearances, he was often booed. On voting day, people threw stink bombs at his car.

Roosevelt won the election by a landslide – only six of the forty-eight states voted for Hoover. The result was: Hoover 15,759,000 votes; Roosevelt 22,810,000 votes. The concept map below outlines reasons for Hoover's defeat.

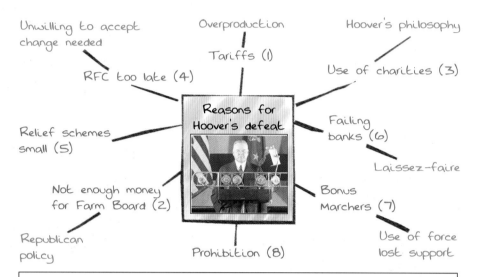

Unwilling to accept change needed

RFC too late (4)

Relief schemes small (5)

Not enough money for Farm Board (2)

Republican policy

Overproduction

Tariffs (1)

Reasons for Hoover's defeat

Prohibition (8)

Hoover's philosophy

Use of charities (3)

Failing banks (6)

Laissez-faire

Bonus Marchers (7)

Use of force lost support

NOTES
1. Hawley–Smoot tariff kept custom duties high on imports. This reduced exports, but industry continued to produce goods.
2. Farm Board did not help all farmers with their debts and caused some resentment.
3. Reliance on charities for help with the unemployed — Hoover naïve in thinking this would solve huge scale problems.
4. RFC (Reconstructon Finance Corporation) introduced too late to make an immediate impact.
5. Relief and government schemes were too small in scope.
6. Banks and businesses continued to fail and confidence fell away.
7. Treatment of the Bonus Marchers caused many to drift away from Hoover.
8. Impact of Prohibition on farmers and the increase in crime lost Hoover more support.

Source G: From Roosevelt's biography by A P Hatch. Here, Hatch is describing part of Roosevelt's campaign tour	Source H: Frances Perkins, Roosevelt's Secretary for Labour after 1933, writing in 1946 about the 1932 campaign
They waited for him in stadiums at fair grounds and on little station platforms – and he hastened happily to greet them. Roosevelt made about twenty speeches a day and made a thousand friends every day. Each time the train stopped he went out on the rear platform for a word and a joke with the cheering crowd.	*In the campaign, Roosevelt saw thousands of Americans. He liked going around the country. His personal relationship with the crowds was on a warm simple level of friendly neighbourly exchange of affection.*

Source J: From a speech Roosevelt made during the presidential campaign, outlining his solutions if he were elected

Our greatest primary task is to put people to work. This is no unsolvable problem if we face it wisely and courageously. It can be accomplished in part by the government itself, treating the task as if it were a war, but at the same time, through its employment, accomplishing greatly needed projects to stimulate and reorganise the use of natural resources.

Tasks

4. *Does the evidence of Source H support Source G about support for Roosevelt?*

5. *What message were the Democrats trying to put across about the Republicans in Source I?*

6. *In what ways does Source J help you understand the reasons for Roosevelt's success in the 1932 presidential campaign?*

7. *What can you learn from Source K about Roosevelt's approach to the USA's economic problems?*

8. *After reading the information on pages 94–97, construct a concept map, like the one on page 98, to show why Roosevelt won the 1932 election. Use the sources to focus on the positive side of Roosevelt. Do not use the negative points about Hoover listed in the concept map.*

9. *Design two posters for the 1932 presidential campaign – one for Hoover and one for Roosevelt.*

10. *Describe the key features of the presidential campaign of 1932. (Remember how to answer this type of question? For further guidance, see page 44.)*

Chapter 10 The nature of the New Deal

What were the aims of the New Deal?

Source B: The economic theory put forward by Roosevelt

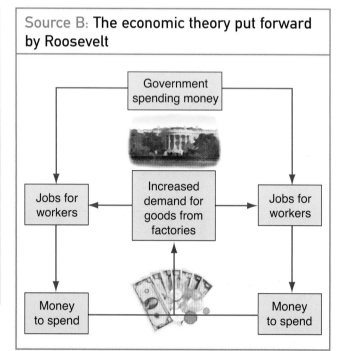

In his nomination speech to the Democratic Party, Roosevelt had promised the American people a 'new deal', and now that he was president it was time to introduce it. His inauguration was crucial in setting out his plans, and within a week of making it, he had received almost 500,000 letters from all over the USA supporting him. He felt it was his task to restore the faith that most Americans had lost in their country. Roosevelt was an experimenter at heart and above all he was receptive to new ideas. He employed Republicans as well as Democrats, conservatives as well as **liberals**, university intellectuals as well as experienced politicians. The aims of the New Deal are set out in the table below.

Relief	• Assist in the removal of poverty • Provide food for the starving • Intervene to prevent people from losing homes/farms
Recovery	• Ensure that the economy was boosted so that people could be given jobs
Reform	• Ensure that there were **welfare** provisions in the future to help the unemployed, old, sick, disabled and the destitute.

The aims of the New Deal.

Tasks

1. *Can you suggest reasons why Roosevelt's inauguration speech (Source A) was liked by so many Americans?*

2. *Look at Source B. How was Roosevelt's approach to the economy different from Hoover's? Explain your answer.*

5. *Imagine you are the governor of a state which has industrial and agricultural workers. Write a letter to President Roosevelt indicating why his proposed solutions to the Depression will help these people.*

6. *Describe the key features of Roosevelt's aims for ending the Depression. (Remember how to answer this type of question? For further guidance, see page 44.)*

What were the 'Hundred Days'?

After his inauguration, Roosevelt set to work immediately. He attacked the problems of the Great Depression and pushed through a huge number of government programmes which aimed to restore the shattered economy. **Congress** met from 9 March until 16 June 1933. This period became known as the Hundred Days. During this time Roosevelt also ended Prohibition (see page 49). On 12 March 1933 he joked, 'I think this would be a good time for a beer.'

The table below shows the most important of the Alphabet Agencies, the various organisations that Roosevelt set up during the Hundred Days,

Task

1. *Look at the table on this page describing the key activities of the Hundred Days. Divide the activities into three groups, as below, and decide in which group the activities should be placed. If you need to, look at the table on page 100 about the three aims of relief, recovery and reform. What do you notice about your decisions?*

Relief	Recovery	Reform

Emergency Banking Act (EBA)	To restore confidence in the banking system. Part of the act prevented banks from investing savings deposits in the **stock market**, which was too unpredictable to guarantee the safety of those funds.
Federal Emergency Relief Administration (FERA)	Emergency relief and funds of $500 million were provided for the unemployed. It was a temporary measure because Roosevelt did not want his opponents to think the government was just handing out money to the unemployed.
Civilian Conservation Corps (CCC)	Designed to tackle unemployment: men between the ages of 18 and 25 were offered work in conservation projects. The workers planted trees, to prevent soil erosion. By the start of the war, more than two million men had been granted some work with the CCC.
National Recovery Administration (NRA)	This agency was to set fair prices, wages and working conditions. Participants displayed the Blue Eagle emblem. The National Industrial Recovery Act (NIRA), which established the NRA, was removed by the Supreme Court in 1935 (see page 108).
Tennessee Valley Authority (TVA)	A huge area covering several states was to be singled out and re-developed. The Tennessee Valley was a poor, backward area which had suffered erosion and flooding. The aim was to resolve these problems and create a prosperous agricultural area.
Home Owner's Loan Act and Home Owner's Loan Corporation (HOLC)	This provided low-interest loans to assist mortgage repayments.
Agricultural Adjustment Act (AAA)	Aimed to increase farm prices and in some cases did so by ploughing up crops and slaughtering animals (see page 105). Prices did rise slowly. The Supreme Court rejected the Act in 1936.
Farm Credit Administration (FCA)	Money was made available to assist farmers with their mortgages and this saved many from eviction. Twenty per cent of farmers benefited from the scheme.
Public Works Administration (PWA)	Monies were made available for huge-scale public works. $3300 million was spent by this agency.
Reconstruction Finance Corporation (RFC)	Hoover's agency was retained (see page 77) but Roosevelt pumped in more money. Banks and businesses were able to use some of the $15 billion pumped in by Roosevelt to begin the process of investment once again.

The banking crisis

The most important task waiting for Roosevelt at the beginning of the Hundred Days was stemming the crisis in banking. More than 2000 banks had closed in the twelve months before he had become president, and if there was to be any confidence in the banking and commercial sectors, people had to feel that they could save and invest without fear of huge financial losses.

Furthermore, those who were saving in banks were withdrawing money at an alarming rate, thus undermining the whole banking system. Roosevelt closed all banks for ten days and then, on the radio (with 60 million people listening to him), explained his plans – he would allow those banks with assets to re-open and those without would be closed until he and his advisers put forward a rescue programme. He assured people that money was safer in a bank than at home. When the banks re-opened, people no longer wished to withdraw their savings, and many put back what had recently been withdrawn. Roosevelt had brought back confidence in the system.

His radio talk became the first of many 'fireside chats' (see Sources A, B and C).

Source C: Cartoon of Roosevelt giving a 'fireside chat', 1933

A MAN TALKING TO HIS FRIENDS

Source A: From Roosevelt's first 'fireside chat', 12 March 1933

Some of our bankers have shown themselves either incompetent or dishonest in their handling of the people's funds. They had used money . . . in speculations and unwise loans. Confidence and courage are the essentials in our plan . . . you must not be stampeded by rumours . . . Together we cannot fail.

Source B: From *The Roosevelt I Knew* by Frances Perkins, 1946

When he broadcast I realised how clearly his mind focused on the people listening at the other end. As he talked his head would nod and his hands would move in simple, natural, comfortable gestures. His face would smile and light up as though he were actually sitting on the front porch or in the kitchen with them. People felt this and it bound them to him in affection.

Source D: From The New Deal by D Brogan, 1968, describing the impression Roosevelt made on people

In his fireside chats on the radio, he projected himself and his message into millions of homes. Most years he made extensive tours and hundreds of thousands saw for themselves that big smile, the jauntily cocked cigarette holder, glasses and jutting jaw made famous by photographs and cartoons.

Tasks

2. What was the intention of the activity of the Hundred Days?

3. Look at Sources A, B, C and D. Explain why the 'fireside chats' were important for Roosevelt.

4. *Explain how Roosevelt changed the role of the government in the Hundred Days. (Remember how to answer this type of question? For further guidance, see page 93.)*

Unemployment

Roosevelt asked Congress for legislation to help the unemployed. He wanted legislation that would involve government in direct relief, provide money for roads, dams, schools and other public works projects and set up various programmes to put as many young unemployed people as possible to work.

Civilian Conservation Corps (CCC)

The Civilian Conservation Corps was set up to create jobs for the many men who were **hobos** or living in Hoovervilles. Among the first recruits were several thousand members of the Bonus Army. CCC workers received food, clothing and one dollar per day. This scheme was quite popular, as Source E describes. By August 1933 there were about 250,000 working on the CCC.

> **Source E:** From *Newsweek* magazine, 8 April 1933, describing the intent of the CCC
>
> *A new army of pioneers will go into the woods within a few weeks. Across 150,000,000 acres of forest lands ... will march an army of workers who are at the moment unemployed and trudging the streets. It is clear that this army will be fully enlisted because applications have rained into Washington from all over the country.*

Workers in the Civilian Conservation Corps. Can you suggest reasons why some Americans criticised the CCC?

Federal Emergency Relief Administration (FERA)

FERA was authorised to distribute $500 million through grants to state and local agencies for relief. Neither Congress nor the people really liked the idea of Americans being given money by the government or states and as a result, on 8 November, Congress passed legislation forming the Civil Works Administration to create public jobs. FERA was led by Harry Hopkins, an experienced administrator and social worker.

Civil Works Administration (CWA)

By January 1934, about four million Americans, mostly unskilled workers, were on the CWA's payroll. The Works Progress Administration replaced the CWA in 1935, and over the years it employed more than eight million people. Some of the workers built roads, but on occasions this agency was laughed at for creating jobs such as scaring birds away from buildings or sweeping leaves in parks.

	Unemployed in millions	Percentage of workforce unemployed
1933	12.8	24.9
1934	11.3	21.7
1935	10.6	20.1

Unemployment, 1933–35.

Tasks

5. *What can you learn from Source E about the setting up of the CCC?*

6. *Why do you think that members of the Bonus Army were amongst the first recruits to the CCC?*

7. *Study the table on unemployment above. What conclusions can be drawn about the New Deal in its first two years of operation?*

Industry

Roosevelt was determined to increase the productivity of American industry. To help industry recover, the National Industrial Recovery Act (NIRA) was passed.

Source F: **A cartoon published in a newspaper in 1933: 'The Spirit of the New Deal'.**

National Industrial Recovery Act

Part of the NIRA was the National Recovery Administration (NRA). This sought to have employers draw up common codes of employment such as maximum hours and **minimum wages**. In the 1920s some groups of employers had got together to fix wages/prices, and it was hoped that these codes would end the fierce competition which had resulted in wage levels being reduced.

To encourage business leaders to comply with the codes, the NRA launched a publicity campaign – it adopted as its symbol a blue eagle poster and asked people to buy only goods from businesses displaying the poster. The people did rally to this call, and the symbol of the blue eagle (see Source F) appeared all over the country.

Source G: **From A New Jersey factory notice board, 1933, showing workers what needed to be done to stimulate the economy**

President Roosevelt has done his part; now you do something. Buy something – buy anything, paint your kitchen, send a telegram, give a party, get a car, pay a bill, rent a flat, fix your roof, build a house … It doesn't matter what you do – but get going and keep going. This old world is starting to move.

Source H: **From one of Roosevelt's fireside chats, June 1933. He was talking about employers paying fair wages**

If all employers in each competitive group agree to pay their workers the same reasonable wages – and require the same hours – reasonable hours – then higher wages will hurt no employer. Such action is better for the employer than unemployment and low wages, because it makes more buyers for his product. That is the simple idea which is at the very heart of the Industrial Recovery Act.

Source I: **Earnings and prices in the USA, 1920–41. The year 1926 is taken as the base line**

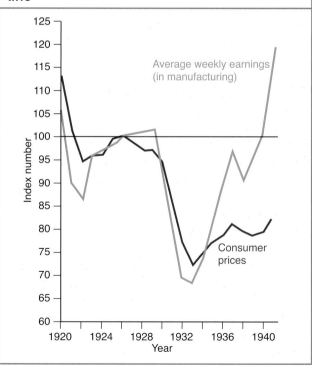

Source K: Cotton being ploughed back into the ground

Agriculture

Roosevelt was aware that farmers had experienced several years of low prices and poor profits. He was keen to introduce measures which would have an immediate effect and ensure that farmers would be able to carry out their work without making losses. Consequently, the Farm Credit Administration and Agricultural Administration were introduced.

Farm Credit Administration (FCA)
- Twenty per cent of farmers used the funds offered by government.
- Low-interest loans were made readily available to farmers to help them pay of their debts.

Agricultural Adjustment Act (AAA)
This proved to be rather controversial. It was set up to increase farmers' incomes but it was decided that, to achieve this, production levels would have to drop. As production fell, prices would rise and farmers could begin to recover. Farmers would be paid by the government to grow less.

- More than five million pigs were killed, and thousands of hectares of cotton were ploughed back into the ground.
- Though many hungry people did not understand the logic of destroying animals and not using them, farmers were generally satisfied with the policy because prices did begin to rise.
- By 1936, incomes were one and a half times higher than they had been in 1933.

Tasks

8. *Look at the information and photograph on page 103 and Sources E (page 103) and F (page 104). Do you think Roosevelt was successful in achieving his New Deal aims on unemployment? Draw up a balance sheet – on one side list successes and on the other failures. Explain your points carefully.*

9. *What does Source J tell us about the New Deal? (Remember how to answer this type of question? For further guidance, see page 26.)*

10. *Does Source H support Source G on the question of how to solve the problems facing US industry?*

11. *What does Source I show you about the New Deal? Explain your answer. (When using the graph, look for such things as quick/slow increases, increases which double or treble, and inconsistencies.)*

12. *Explain why Roosevelt introduced the Alphabet Agencies. (Remember how to answer this type of question? For further guidance, see page 74.)*

13. *Look at Sources J and K. Explain why many people at this time were horrified by the killing of large numbers of animals and the ploughing back of crops.*

14. *Was Roosevelt a friend to the farmers? Explain your answer.*

The Tennessee Valley Authority (TVA)

Source L: From *TVA: Adventure in Planning* by J Huxley, 1943. Huxley had surveyed the Tennessee Valley in the early 1930s

The erosion was appalling. Here before me, was the basic productivity of an area being stripped from a vast region and being taken to the sea by the river. I saw outcrops of bare rock which three generations ago had been covered with rich soil over a metre in depth. The amount of soil annually washed or blown out of the USA is estimated at three million tons.

Task

15. *What does Source L show us about the problems that farmers faced in the Tennessee Valley area?*

One of the most important features of the New Deal was the establishment of the Tennessee Valley Authority (TVA). The Tennessee Valley was one of the most depressed regions of the USA. More than half the population of 2.5 million were receiving relief, and few people had electricity. Annual flood damage (the result of erosion caused by de-forestation) was put at $1.75 million.

Hence, if this area could be re-invigorated, then Roosevelt could show that his policies were clearly aimed at benefiting the country. Furthermore, it was hoped that immediate improvements could be made in the area. The TVA was to be an independent public body which would have control of government property at Muscle Shoals, Tennessee.

The scope of the TVA was immense and it aimed not only to regenerate the region but also to create jobs. It was to be responsible for generating and distributing electric power for that area by means of the creation of a system of dams which would enable flood control. The many dams meant there would be reservoirs and power plants, and it was hoped that with cheap electricity and an end to flooding, industry would be attracted to the area.

The success of the TVA

The Authority would also develop river navigation and the manufacture and distribution of fertiliser to farmers in order to re-establish the area. The TVA had the power to build recreation areas, as well as to provide health and welfare facilities. Eventually, the activities of the TVA covered seven states, 104,000 square kilometres (see map) with a population of seven million people, and it did prove to be one of the successes of the New Deal.

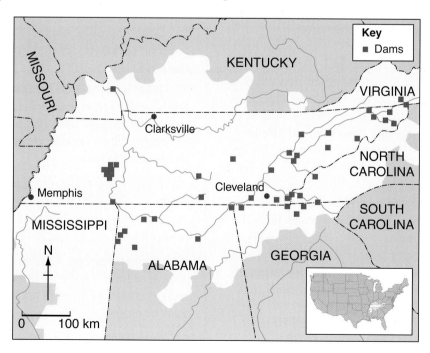

Map of the Tennessee Valley area.

The Norris Dam, one of 30 TVA sites. This was part of a network which helped generate electricity for the TVA.

Opposition to the TVA

The TVA was not received well by everyone – farmers whose land was flooded were of course opponents, as were some big business owners who felt that the USA was moving towards becoming a socialist state. These business people campaigned against other areas of the USA being given similar treatment to the Tennessee Valley.

The TVA is still in existence today.

Tasks

16. *Write a 'fireside chat' for Roosevelt, explaining why he is introducing the TVA scheme.*

17. *Write a speech for some business people showing why the TVA is a sign that President Roosevelt is taking the USA down the road to a socialist state and why it should be opposed.*

18. *Draw a concept map about the TVA like the one opposite. On the first layer, insert the reasons for setting up the TVA. On the second layer, insert the solutions to the problems. Put the reasons in one colour and the solutions in another. This will help you to see whether you have completed the task correctly.*

19. *Describe the key features of the successes of the TVA. (Remember how to answer this type of question? For further guidance, see page 44.)*

20. *Explain the effects of the Alphabet Agencies on US agriculture. (Remember how to answer this type of question? For further guidance, see page 52.)*

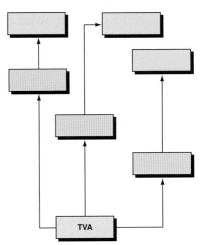

What was the Second New Deal?

Source A: **From 'The New Deal in review, 1936–40' in** *New Republic*, **a US magazine, May 1940**

The New Deal has done far more for the general welfare of the country and its citizens than any administration in the previous history of the nation. Its relief for the underprivileged in city and country has been indispensable. Without this relief an appalling amount of misery would have resulted ... the New Deal has accomplished much of permanent benefit to the nation.

The New Deal continued into 1934, and Roosevelt received criticism for not doing enough to reduce unemployment, and criticism for doing too much and increasing the role of government (see Chapter 11). About ten million were still unemployed, and he was aware that he would have to show some successes, because presidential elections were approaching. In January 1935, in his yearly message to Congress, Roosevelt introduced his second New Deal, a broad programme of reform to help farmers, workers, the poor and the unemployed.

The Works Progress Administration (WPA)

The WPA was a scheme headed by Harry Hopkins, who had been in charge of FERA (see page 103). He was quick to put the programme into action. The mainstay of the programme was funding and building projects, including hospitals, schools, airports, harbours, etc, thus creating employment. Its other responsibilities included:

- overseeing a $4.8 billion relief programme
- putting unemployed teachers back to work by creating the Adult Education Programme
- creating community service schemes to employ artists, writers and actors.

Both directly and indirectly, the WPA improved the quality of life in communities across the USA. In all, during its five years of operation, it gave work to more than eight million people and spent $11 billion. Roosevelt described the work of the WPA as 'priming the pump' – in other words, the government was acting by re-starting the economic machinery.

National Labour Relations Act

Roosevelt was keen to protect the rights of workers, and when the NIRA was removed in 1935 he sought another approach. In the same year he was able to bring in the Wagner Act (or National Labour Relations Act):

- The Act upheld the right of workers to organise and enter into **collective bargaining**. In 1933, there were three million trade union members and in 1939, more than nine million.
- The Wagner Act set up the National Labour Relations Board, which was given power to act against employers who used unfair practices, such as sacking workers who had joined a union.

The business community opposed the Wagner Act and complained that it had defined unfair practices for employers, but not for workers.

Fair Labour Standards Act

Further improvements came with the Fair Labour Standards Act in 1938. By this Act:

- Minimum wages and maximum hours were established for all employees of businesses engaged in interstate commerce.
- 300,000 secured higher wages as a result and more than one million had a shorter working week.
- Child labour was not permitted except on farms.

Social Security Act

Perhaps the most important reform was the Social Security Act of 1935. By this Act, the government at last accepted its direct responsibility for meeting the basic needs of its citizens. The Act:

- Established pension benefits for the elderly, the orphaned and those injured in industrial accidents. Pensions were for those over 65, and the funding would be met by a tax on employers and workers.
- Established unemployment benefits, which would be funded by a tax on the payrolls of employers.

- Set up the Social Security Board to administer payments.

Some of Roosevelt's critics said that the act did not go far enough, mainly because the benefits were too small. However, there were critics who said the act would ruin the USA because it would discourage people from saving and using their initiative, and make them depend on the government for handouts.

Source B: A cartoon drawn in 1933, called 'You remembered me'. Roosevelt is shown shaking hands with 'The Forgotten Man'

Source C: A cartoon: 'Roosevelt the friend of the poor'

Tasks

1. Study Source A. Do you agree that the New Deal 'accomplished much of permanent benefit'?

2. Study Source B.
- What do you think the cartoonist meant by the phrase 'You remembered me'?
- What can you learn about the role of Roosevelt from this source?

3. Explain why the Social Security Act is such a significant piece of legislation in US history.

4. In what ways does Source C show that Roosevelt did not follow the idea of 'rugged individualism'?

5. Explain how Roosevelt was able to appeal to various sections of US society.
(Remember how to answer this type of question? For further guidance, see page 93.)

Reforming Acts

Equally significant were the reforming acts, which restricted the activities of banks. Following the Emergency Banking Act, further changes were made. Among the most important measures were the Securities Act and the Banking Act. The Securities Act was designed to eliminate fraud in the stock market. Under this law, a company which deliberately deceived investors about its financial status could be sued. The Banking Act prohibited banks from investing savings in the stock market, which was too unpredictable to assure the safety of these funds.

Achievements

The New Deal had notable positive achievements to its credit: the transformation of the Tennessee Valley, the PWA and the WPA. But far more significant was the simple fact that the New Deal restored hope to millions of men and women by providing them with a job or saving their home.

By 1937, Roosevelt had won a second term and there was a reduction in the amount of legislation emerging from Congress. However, 1937 and 1938 saw the USA experience another period of **recession**. Roosevelt had decided to cut back on government spending in these years, but he changed his mind, and in June 1938 Congress passed another huge spending bill. Unemployment did fall after 1939 (the year when Roosevelt said the New Deal was at an end), but it did not return to pre-1929 levels until the USA was involved in the Second World War.

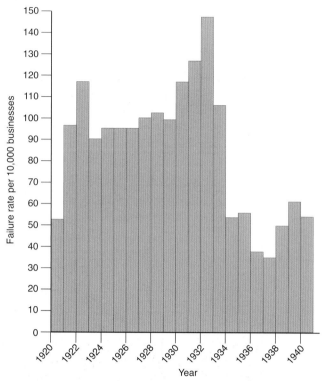

Graph showing business failures, 1920–40.

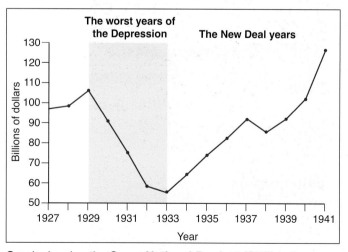

Graph showing the **Gross National Product** (GNP) in the USA, 1927–41. GNP is the total value of all goods and services produced in a country in one year.

Tasks

6. *Explain the effects of the Second New Deal on the lives of US citizens. (Remember how to answer this type of question? For further guidance, see page 52.)*

7. *'Roosevelt was successful with the Second New Deal.' Use the information on pages 108–110, including the sources and graphs, as well as your own knowledge, to construct an argument agreeing or disagreeing with this view.*

8. *First re-read this whole chapter (pages 95–112). Then construct a concept map of how Roosevelt tried to tackle the problems of the Depression. First, draw a central box and write 'Depression' in it. Then draw arrows leading out of the central box. On each arrow write a problem caused by the Depression. Finally draw a box at the end of each arrow. In these boxes write details of how Roosevelt tried to solve each problem.*

These photographs are 'before' and 'after' shots of an area in Tennessee Valley, where the planting of trees successfully halted land erosion.

What was Roosevelt's role in the recovery?

Source A: From *Franklin D. Roosevelt and the New Deal* by W. Leuchtenburg, 1963

When Roosevelt toured the country in 1936, thousands of men and women pressed up to the railroad tracks for a glimpse of the President . . . He could hear people crying out: 'He saved my home', 'He saved my job.'

Chapters 11 and 12 explore the opposition to the New Deal and the successes and failures of that opposition. By now you will have concluded that many people voted for Roosevelt because they were impressed by his spirit of optimism. He seemed to care about the ordinary man and woman. He made sure that he was seen across the USA during the presidential campaign of 1932. Even when he became president, he was careful to keep in touch with people by means of his 'fireside chats'. He was admired for his honesty and always said he would explain any crisis that befell the USA.

Evidence of Roosevelt's success and popularity can be found in the result of the 1936 presidential election – which he won by a massive margin. He gained a majority of votes in 46 of the 48 states.

Source B: A US cartoon of 1933

Source C: From the song 'We've Got Franklin D. Roosevelt Back Again', written shortly after the 1936 presidential election.

Since Roosevelt's been re-elected, we'll not be neglected
Good old times are coming back again
You can laugh and tell a joke, you can dance and drink and smoke
No more standing in the blowing, snowing rain
He's got things in full swing, we're all working and getting our pay
We've got Franklin D. Roosevelt back again
Since Roosevelt's been re-elected
Moon liquor's been corrected
We've got Franklin D. Roosevelt back again

Tasks

1. What do the following phrases in the song mean?

- 'we'll not be neglected'
- 'no more standing in the rain'
- 'moon liquor's been corrected'

2. Write your own poem or song about why many Americans wanted Roosevelt as president.

3. Was Roosevelt's personal attraction the main reason why Americans wanted him as president in the 1930s? Explain your answer.

You may use the following information to help you with your answer.

- Roosevelt's personal attraction
- Failure of Hoover
- Alphabet Agencies
- Social reforms

(For further guidance on how to answer this type of question, see page 119.)

4. What can you learn from Source B about Roosevelt and the New Deal?

Opposition to the New Deal

Source A: 'Ring Around A Roosevelt, Pockets Full of Dough': a cartoonist's view of the New Deal. From the *Washington Post*, May 1938

Tasks

Study Source A.

1. What message is the cartoonist trying to put across about the New Deal?

2. How does the cartoonist get across this message?

The New Deal was not popular with all citizens of the USA. Indeed, there was opposition from a number of individuals such as Huey Long, Dr Frances Townsend and Father Charles Coughlin. In addition some groups such as Republicans, businessmen and even some of Roosevelt's own party, the Democrats, were critical of the New Deal. However, possibly the most serious opposition came from the Supreme Court who believed Roosevelt was acting **unconstitutionally**.

This chapter answers the following questions:

• Why did some individuals oppose the New Deal?
• Why did the Supreme Court oppose the New Deal?
• Why did some politicians oppose the New Deal?

Examination skills

This chapter gives guidance on answering question 3 from Unit 2. This question, which is worth sixteen marks, is a scaffolding question.

Why did some individuals oppose the New Deal?

The New Deal attracted opposition from certain prominent individuals who believed that Roosevelt was not doing enough. They had their own ideas about what he should be doing. The three most important were:

- Governor Huey Long
- Father Charles Coughlin
- Dr Francis Townsend

Who were these three men, what ideas did they have and why did they oppose the New Deal? The answers to these questions can be found in the following fact files.

Huey Long

CONFIDENTIAL

NAME: Huey Long, 1893–1935

Huey Long had been Governor of the State of Louisiana, ruling it almost as a dictator. Nevertheless, he had shown genuine concern for the state's poor. He taxed the wealthy, especially the oil companies, to pay for improvements such as new bridges across rivers, roads across swamps, and new schools. In other words, he had a track record of helping the less privileged.

Long claimed that Roosevelt had failed to share out the nation's wealth fairly and he announced his own plans to do this under the slogan 'Share Our Wealth'. Long said that Roosevelt should confiscate the 'swollen fortunes' of the wealthy and use this to give every American family a house, a car and two or three thousand dollars a year.

He promised to make 'every man a king' and attracted the support of millions of the poor. Membership of 'Share Our Wealth' clubs reached 7.5 million votes in the 1936 presidential election.

He was killed by a doctor whose career he had ruined. Long's bodyguard fired 61 bullets into the doctor who still managed to fire the one shot that killed Long.

CONFIDENTIAL

NAME: Father Charles Coughlin, 1891–1979

At first, in 1933, Coughlin supported Roosevelt but within two years he was an opponent, setting up the National Union for Social Justice. This organisation promised work and fair wages for all. He also proposed to nationalise all banks and introduce a national minimum wage.

Coughlin criticised the New Deal for not doing enough and labelled Roosevelt as 'anti-God' because he was not really helping the needy. His main influence came from his weekly broadcasts which attracted over 40 million listeners, especially from urban and lower middle-class America. However, many more people listened to Roosevelt's 'fireside chats'(see page 102).

Father Charles Coughlin

CONFIDENTIAL

NAME: Dr Francis Townsend, 1867–1960

Townsend gained much support from old people who, in 1934, had benefited little from the New Deal. He set up an organisation called 'Old Age Revolving Pension Plan', also known as the Townsend clubs, which had attracted five million members by 1935.

He proposed to introduce a 2 per cent tax on business transactions and the money raised would be used to finance his scheme. The scheme was to give $200 a month to every citizen over 60 who had retired. The plan was to encourage more people to retire and thus create more jobs for the unemployed. The scheme collapsed in 1936 when Townsend's business partner was found guilty of stealing from the funds.

Dr Francis Townsend

Source A: Texas poster advertising Townsend's old age pensions plan, photo taken in 1935

Tasks

1. *Source A shows a poster advertising Townsend's scheme. Draw a similar poster advertising the scheme put forward by either Long or Coughlin.*

2. *What can you learn about the weaknesses of the New Deal from the schemes introduced by these three individuals?*

3. *Explain why Long, Coughlin and Townsend opposed the New Deal. (Remember how to answer this type of question? For further guidance, see page 74.)*

4. *Which of the three individuals do you think provided the most serious opposition to Roosevelt and the New Deal? Give at least one reason for your choice.*

Why did the Supreme Court oppose the New Deal?

In many respects the Supreme Court provided the most serious opposition to the New Deal and did much to handicap Roosevelt's measures.

The Supreme Court's Republican nature

One reason that the Supreme Court opposed some of Roosevelt's measures was that it was dominated by Republican judges. This was because from 1861 to 1933 there were only sixteen years of Democrat presidents and few opportunities to nominate Democrat judges.

Out of the sixteen cases concerning the 'Alphabet Agencies' which were tried by the Supreme Court in 1935 and 1936, the judges declared that in eleven, Roosevelt had acted unconstitutionally. In reality, he was using central or federal powers which the Constitution had not given him. Two cases show the opposition he faced.

The 'Sick Chickens' case, 1935

This involved four brothers, the Schechters, who ran a poultry business. In 1933 they signed the National Industrial Recovery Administration (NIRA) rules of fair prices, wages and competition. In 1935, the NIRA took them to court for selling a batch of diseased chickens unfit for human consumption. The Schechters appealed to the Supreme Court, which declared the NIRA illegal because its activities were unconstitutional. It gave the federal government powers it should not have to interfere in state affairs, in this case the state of New York. As a result, 750 of the NIRA codes were immediately scrapped.

The US v Butler case, 1936

In this case the Supreme Court declared the Agricultural Adjustment Act illegal. The judges decided that giving help to farmers was a matter for each state government, not the federal government. As a result all help to farmers ceased.

The Supreme Court

The American Constitution set up the Supreme Court to keep a check on both Congress and the president. It consists of nine judges, appointed for life, whose task it is to make sure laws passed by Congress are not unconstitutional (that is, they do not break the Constitution). When a judge dies or retires, a new judge is nominated by the president.

Source A: **A cartoon of 1936 showing Roosevelt lassoing a Supreme Court judge**

THE LINE OF LEAST RESISTANCE

Roosevelt's attempts at reform

After his massive victory in the 1936 presidential election, Roosevelt decided that public opinion was behind his New Deal. Therefore in February 1937, he threatened to retire those judges in the Supreme Court who were over 70 and replace them with younger ones who supported his policies.

These attempts failed for two reasons. First, many saw this move as unconstitutional. As they saw it, the president was trying to destroy the position of the Supreme Court by packing it with his own supporters. Second, Roosevelt failed to consult senior members of his own party. One particular group, the **Conservative Democrats** – who came from the South and represented farming areas – strongly opposed Roosevelt's proposed reform of the Supreme Court.

Nevertheless, in March/April 1937 the Supreme Court reversed the 'Sick Chickens' decision and accepted Roosevelt's Social Security Act, which brought in old age pensions and unemployment insurance (see pages 108–109). On the other hand, the whole episode had damaged Roosevelt's reputation and lost him the support of some members of his own party.

Tasks

1. Study Source A. What is the message of the cartoon?

2. Explain the effects the Supreme Court had on the New Deal.
   (Remember how to answer this type of question? For further guidance, see page 52.)

3. Was Roosevelt right to reform the Supreme Court?

   Make a copy of the following table and write reasons in both columns.

Roosevelt right to reform Supreme Court	Roosevelt wrong to reform Supreme Court

   Now look at the completed table. On balance, do you think he was right?

4. You are one of Roosevelt's leading advisers in 1936. What advice would you give him about the Supreme Court? Write your advice in the form of a memo. Here is how you could set it out. Remember to fill in the information at the start of your memo.

Memo	
To:	From:
Date:	Subject:

   Dear Mr President,
   I ....

Why did some politicians oppose the New Deal?

Republicans and businessmen

The Republicans strongly opposed the New Deal. Not only were they traditional opponents of the Democrats, they were also the party representing the interests of America's rich families and large corporations. These believed that Roosevelt was doing too much to help people and was changing the accepted role of government in the USA.

The American Liberty League

This group, set up in 1934 to preserve individual freedom, was backed by wealthy businessmen. Two of them, Alfred Smith and John Davis, had – rather surprisingly – previously stood as Democrat presidential candidates.

Democrats

Even the Conservative Democrats – members of Roosevelt's own party – opposed the New Deal. They were especially against the Wagner Act (see page 108), which had given greater powers to the trade unions.

A cartoon from the *Philadelphia Enquirer*, 1936. What message is the cartoonist trying to get across?

Tasks

1. *Explain why there was opposition from some politicians to the New Deal. (Remember how to answer this type of question? For further guidance, see page 74.)*

2. *On the right is a concept map showing some of the reasons for the opposition of Republicans and many businessmen to the New Deal. However, some boxes are not completed.*

- *Copy the concept map.*
- *See if you can find other reasons for opposition from these groups. You may get clues from Chapter 10 (pages 95–112).*
- *Complete the blank boxes.*
- *Add extra boxes if you find even more reasons.*

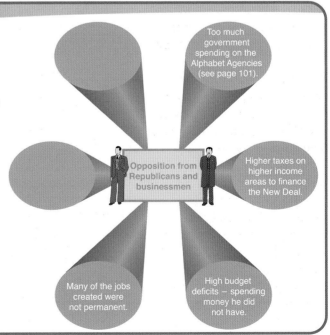

Examination practice

This section provides guidance on how to answer question 3 from Unit 2, which is worth sixteen marks – the most for any question. This is the scaffolding question because you are given four points (a 'scaffold') around which to build your essay answer.

Question – scaffolding

Was the most serious opposition to the New Deal from the Supreme Court?

> You may use the following information to help you with your answer.
>
> - The opposition of the Supreme Court
> - Opposition from some politicians
> - Huey Long
> - Father Charles Coughlin

(16 marks)

How to answer

- Ensure you do not simply describe the four parts of the scaffolding.
- Focus on the key words in the question, such as key dates, events and the main theme. This question is about opposition to the New Deal.
- Make use of at least three points of the scaffolding or develop at least three points of your own. The examiner will have assisted you by placing the points in chronological or topical order.
- You can make use of the scaffolding or add one or more points of your own not mentioned in the scaffolding – Frances Townsend, for example. Make it clear to the examiner that you are doing this.
- Remember to make a judgement about the importance of each factor and then an overall judgement at the end.
- Write an introduction that identifies the key areas you are going to explain in your answer.
- Write a conclusion which gives your overall judgement on the question. Remember, you need to make a decision on the relative importance of the points. You could decide that they were all equally important or two were more important. Give a reason for your judgement.

The sample on page 120 shows the steps you should take to write a good answer to a scaffolding question. Use the steps and examples to complete the answer to the question by writing the paragraphs on the scaffolding factors and linking them where possible. Alternatively you could use the grid to the right to structure your answer to the question. However, you could also use points of your own rather than the scaffolding factors.

INTRODUCTION
- Explain the key theme of the question.
- Suggest the key areas you are going to cover in your answer.

FIRST PARAGRAPH – FIRST SCAFFOLDING FACTOR (OR POINT OF YOUR OWN)
- Introduce the first factor.
- Fully explain this factor.
- Make a judgement about the importance of this factor.

SECOND PARAGRAPH – SECOND SCAFFOLDING FACTOR (OR POINT OF YOUR OWN)

THIRD PARAGRAPH – THIRD SCAFFOLDING FACTOR (OR POINT OF YOUR OWN)

FOURTH PARAGRAPH – FOURTH FACTOR
This could be an additional factor mentioned in the scaffolding or a point of your own.

CONCLUSION
- Begin with 'Overall . . . '
- Make a final judgement on the relative importance of all the factors.

Examination practice

Example:
In the years 1933–41 Roosevelt introduced a series of measures, known as the New Deal, to reduce the worst effects of the Depression. Although popular with many US citizens, this New Deal did arouse opposition from some politicians, a few key individuals and the Supreme Court.

STEP 1
Write an introduction that identifies the key issues you need to cover in your answer and your main argument.

Example:
The Supreme Court opposed the New Deal – in particular the powers being used by Roosevelt to carry out the New Deal.

STEP 2
Introduce the first factor. This could be the factor mentioned in the question or a point of your own.

Example:
This opposition was partly due to the fact that the Supreme Court was dominated by Republican judges but also because the Court was convinced that Roosevelt was acting unconstitutionally. For example, out of the sixteen cases which were tried by the Supreme Court in 1935 and 1936, the judges declared that in eleven, Roosevelt had acted unconstitutionally. In other words, he was using central or federal powers which the Constitution had not given him. Two famous cases brought against Roosevelt, and supported by the Supreme Court were the 'Sick Chickens' case, 1935, and, the following year, the US v Butler case.

STEP 3
Fully explain the factor.

Example:
The Supreme Court provided serious opposition to the New Deal because they were successful in overturning some of the measures, particularly of the NRA and the AAA. Roosevelt tried, unsuccessfully, to change the membership of the Supreme Court and these attempts damaged his reputation as president.

STEP 4
Make a judgement on the importance of this factor.

Now have a go yourself at the next two factors. You may wish to add an additional factor mentioned in the scaffolding or one of your own.

Have a go yourself

Example:
Overall there was opposition to the New Deal from a range of individuals and groups. However, the most serious opposition came from the Supreme Court. The Court forced Roosevelt to make changes to some of his Alphabet Agencies whilst Roosevelt made a serious mistake in trying to bring in his own judges.

STEP 5
Write a conclusion making your final judgement on the question.

12 The extent of recovery

Source A: From *New Deal Thought*, written in 1966 by H Zinn, a historian who was critical of the New Deal

When the reform energies of the New Deal began to wane around 1939 and the Depression was over, the nation was back to its normal state: a permanent army of unemployed and twenty or thirty million poverty-stricken people locked from public view by a prosperous middle class.

Source B: From *America in the Twentieth Century*, written in 1989 by another historian, J Patterson

Roosevelt was concerned about more than improving his own position. He wanted to help ordinary people and he expressed their needs in simple language they could understand. In his 'fireside chats' and his numerous press conferences he put across the image of a man who cared. His air of confidence gave people hope and restored their faith in democracy. His New Deal measures did much to revive the economy and get the country out of its worst depression.

Tasks

1. *What does Source A tell us about the New Deal? (Remember how to answer this type of question? For further guidance, see page 26.)*

2. *Does Source B express the same views? Explain your answer.*

As is clear from Sources A and B, historians disagree about the New Deal. Some believe it was a success. They point out that it reduced unemployment, brought the USA out of Depression and, above all else, gave hope to large numbers of Americans. Others, however, argue that the New Deal provided only temporary and short-term solutions and that it was the Second World War which really got the US economy going again.

This chapter answers the following questions:

- In what ways did the USA recover?
- What were the failures of the New Deal?

Examination skills
This chapter provides the opportunity to practise some of the question types from Unit 2.

The New Deal achieved a number of milestones:

Role of government and the president
- Restored the faith of people in government after the *laissez-faire* approach of Hoover
- Preserved democracy and ensured there was no mass support of right-wing politicians
- Greatly extended the role of central government and the president.

Economy
- Stabilised the US banking system
- Cut the number of business failures
- Greatly improved the **infrastructure** of the USA by providing roads, schools and power stations.

Unemployment
The Alphabet Agencies (see page 101) provided work for millions. Unemployment fell from a peak of 24.9 million in 1933 to 14.3 million four years later.

Industrial workers
The NRA (see page 104) and the Second New Deal (see page 108) greatly strengthened the position of trade unions and made corporations negotiate with them.

Social welfare
The Social Security Act (see page 108) provided the USA with something approaching a welfare state, which provided pensions for the elderly and widows and state help for the sick and disabled.

Black Americans
Around 200,000 black Americans gained benefits from the CCC (see page 103) and other New Deal Agencies. Many benefited from slum clearance programmes and housing projects.

Women
Some women achieved prominent positions under the New Deal:

- Eleanor Roosevelt became an important campaigner for social reform.
- Frances Perkins was the first woman appointed to a cabinet post (she became secretary of labour).

Source A: **A cartoon about the achievements of the NRA, September 1933**

Source B: WPA workers widening a street in 1935.

Source C: A graph showing US national income for the years 1927–41

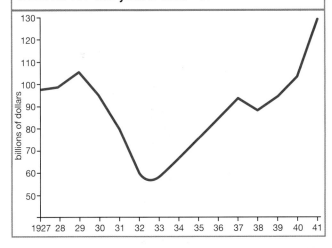

billions of dollars

1927 28 29 30 31 32 33 34 35 36 37 38 39 40 41

Source D: A graph showing the percentage of the workforce out of work in the years 1929–45

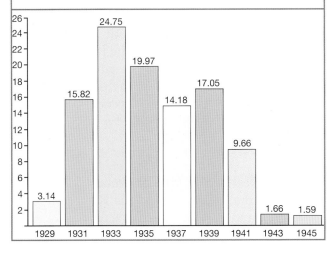

Year	Percentage
1929	3.14
1931	15.82
1933	24.75
1935	19.97
1937	14.18
1939	17.05
1941	9.66
1943	1.66
1945	1.59

Source E: From a letter written to Roosevelt in 1935, explaining the benefits of the New Deal

Dear Mr President,

This is just to tell you everything is all right now. The man you sent found our house all right and we went down to the bank with him and the mortgage can go on for a while longer. You remember we wrote to you about losing the furniture too. Well, your man got it back for us. I never heard of a president like you, Mr Roosevelt.

Tasks

1. *What can you learn from Source A about the New Deal?*

2. *Describe the achievements of the New Deal for industrial workers, black Americans and women. (Remember how to answer this type of question? For further guidance, see page 31.)*

3. *Study Sources B, C, and D. What do they suggest about the achievements of the New Deal?*

4. *Explain the effects that the New Deal had on unemployment. (Remember how to answer this type of question? For further guidance, see page 52.)*

What were the failures of the New Deal?

The New Deal had limitations and shortcomings.

Role of government and the president

The New Deal divided the USA. Roosevelt:
- gave too much power to the federal government and the presidency
- ignored the position of the state governments
- tried to change the membership and role of the Supreme Court
- found that his supporters were even accused of being **communists**.

Economy

- The New Deal provided short-term solutions; it did not solve the underlying economic problems.
- The US economy took longer to recover than those of most European countries. When, in 1937, Roosevelt reduced the New Deal Budget, the country went back into depression.

Unemployment

The Alphabet Agencies provided jobs only in the short term, and people ended up back on the dole. Even when unemployment was at its lowest in 1937, there were still over fourteen million out of work, and the number reached nineteen million the following year. It was the Second World War that brought an end to unemployment.

Industrial workers

Unions were still treated with great suspicion by employers. Many strikes were broken up with brutal violence in the 1930s. Large corporations employed 'heavies' to deal with union leaders.

Social welfare

Some argued that social welfare measures put too much pressure on taxpayers, destroyed self-esteem and the idea of 'rugged individualism', and encouraged people to sponge from the state.

Source A: From a 1932 report by Ernie Pyle, a reporter who travelled throughout the USA

You might truthfully say there is nothing left of western Kansas. There was not a tree, or blade of grass, or a dog or cow, or a human being – nothing whatever, nothing at all but grey raw earth and a few farm houses and barns, sticking up from the dark grey sea like white cattle skeletons on the desert. There was nobody in the houses. The humans had given up and gone. It was death, if I have ever seen death.

Source B: From a 1936 manifesto for the Republican Party

America is in peril. For three long years the New Deal administration has dishonoured the American traditions and betrayed the pledges upon which the Democratic Party sought and received public support. The rights and liberties of American citizens have been violated. It has created a vast multitude of new offices, filled them with its favourites, set up a centralised bureaucracy and sent out swarms of inspectors to harass our people.

Black Americans

- Many New Deal agencies **discriminated** against black people. They got no work, were treated worse than whites or were paid lower wages.
- Roosevelt did little to end **segregation** and discrimination in the deep South. For example, he failed to pass laws against the **lynching** of black Americans in case he alienated Democratic senators representing the southern states. During nearly fifteen years as president, Roosevelt passed only one law for black people.

Women

The New Deal offered little to women:
- Some of the National Industrial Recovery Administration codes of 1933 actually required women to be paid less than men.

- Only 8000 women were employed by the CCC out of 2.75 million involved in the scheme.
- Some state governments tried to avoid social security payments to women by introducing special qualifications.

Source C: A 1937 photograph of black people queuing for relief in front of a famous poster

Source D: A 1933 cartoon shows Roosevelt 'priming the pump'

Extent of recovery

The New Deal did encourage some recovery in the US economy and reduce unemployment.

- The Gross National Product of the USA, which had fallen to under $60 billion in 1933, had reached its 1929 level (nearly $100 billion) by 1940.

- Unemployment, which reached its peak of fourteen million in 1933, fell to just over eight million in 1941.
- There were no significant bank failures after 1934, and far fewer businesses went bankrupt.

However, despite Roosevelt's actions, it was clear by the late 1930s that the revival would be sustained only with regular injections of government money. It was only after 1941, when the USA entered the Second World War and the demand for American goods and foods increased dramatically, that the economy was lifted out of depression.

Tasks

1. *What can you learn from Sources A and B about the New Deal?*

2. *What is the message of Sources C and D?*

3. *Explain why the New Deal was a failure for some people. (Remember how to answer this type of question? For further guidance, see page 74.)*

4. *Read the information on pages 122–125. What opinion would the following people have of the New Deal? Would they see it as a success or a failure – or would they have mixed views? Draw a cartoon representing each, with a speech bubble giving their views.*

- *a trade union leader • the head of a large corporation • a state governor • a black worker • a single woman • an old couple*

5. *What would be your final judgement? Was the New Deal a success or a failure? You could use a concept map to organise your answer.*

6. *Were political divisions the greatest failure of the New Deal? Explain your answer.*

You may use the following information to help you with your answer.

- *Political divisions*
- *Unemployment*
- *The economy*
- *Industrial workers*

(For further guidance on how to answer this type of question, see page 119.)

Revision activities

Key Topic 1: The US economy 1919–29

1. Look at the following causes of the economic boom in the USA in the 1920s. Place them in order of importance, beginning with the most important and ending with the least important. Give a brief explanation of your choice of the most important.
   - Government policies • Technological change
   - First World War • Credit

2. Pair together the following sentences:
   (a) Henry Ford realised much time was wasted by workers finding tools and parts.
   (b) Ford workers soon became bored working on the assembly line.
   (c) Most cars were too expensive for many Americans.
   (d) The car industry greatly benefited other industries.
   (e) The car industry also helped isolated rural communities.
   (f) As much as 90 per cent of petrol and 75 per cent of glass was used by the car industry.
   (g) To keep workers, he doubled their pay and reduced hours of work.
   (h) Farmers could reach local towns in less than half an hour.
   (i) Ford made cars affordable by making one model in one colour.
   (j) He introduced the assembly line.

3. Explain in no more than one sentence what you know about the following:
   - The 'old' industries'
   - Problems in the coal industry
   - Differing wage rates in the USA
   - Fashion and the textile industry

4. Summarise in no more than ten words the importance of the following in 1920s USA:
   - Tariffs
   - Scientific management
   - Rayon

5. Write a paragraph explaining why you agree or disagree with each of the following statements. Put the statements in bubbles.
   - The introduction of tractors was beneficial to farmers.
   - The Fordney-McCumber Act did not help farmers.

6. Look at the following reasons for unemployment in agriculture. Place them in order of importance, beginning with the most important and ending with the least important.
   - Growth of the automobile industry
   - Prohibition
   - Demand for higher wages
   - Dust storms

Key Topic 2: US Society, 1919–29

1. True or false?
   (a) Baseball was the most popular spectator sport of the 1920s.
   (b) Scott Fitzgerald was a famous jazz musician
   (c) Jazz originated with white Americans in the deep south.
   (d) Women were given the vote in 1925.
   (e) The Charleston was a famous dance of the 1920s.
   (f) Charlie Chaplin was the first real star of talkies.
   (g) The first talkie was called *The Jazz Singer*.

2. Explain why each of the following was important in the USA of the 1920s:
   • Flappers • jazz • Hollywood • Babe Ruth

3. This account of Prohibition is by a student who has not revised thoroughly. Rewrite it, correcting the errors.

   > *Moonshiners bought alcohol from the gangsters. The brewing industry suffered and the health of American people worsened in Prohibition. Prohibition was ended by President Roosevelt in 1934. Prohibition was introduced after the Wilson Act 1918 after the Anti-Temperance League had pressured for change. Prohibition was difficult to maintain and people like Woodrow Capone broke the law. Illegal bars called stills were set up and speakeasies were closed down.*

4. Below is part of a mind map showing the effects of Prohibition.

   • Add other reasons to the mind map.
   • Show and explain links between at least two effects.

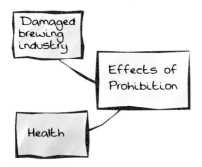

5. Using sketches only, show the importance of the following in the USA of the 1920s:
   • Ku Klux Klan • Monkey Trial
   • Restrictions on immigration

6. Match the question to the answer:

QUESTIONS
   (a) What were the names of the two Italians who were arrested for an armed robbery?
   (b) What was the name given to religious groups in rural areas who opposed Darwin's theory of evolution?
   (c) Who believed that black Americans should return to Africa?
   (d) What was the title of the leader of the Ku Klux Klan?
   (e) What was the 'Red Scare'?

ANSWERS
   (i) Fundamentalists
   (ii) Imperial Wizard
   (iii) Sacco and Vanzetti
   (iv) Marcus Garvey
   (v) Fear of communism

7. Which is the odd one out? Give reasons.
   (a) KKK • NAACP • UNIA
   (b) Darwinism • Scopes • Fundamentalists
   (c) Paul Robeson • Davis Stevenson
      • Countee Cullen

Key Topic 3: The USA in Depression 1929–33

1. Explain, in not more than twenty words for each, the following causes of the Wall Street Crash:
   - Over-speculation
   - Uneven distribution of wealth
   - Overproduction

2. The following account of the Wall Street Crash is by a student has not revised thoroughly. Rewrite it, correcting the errors.

> The Wall Street Crash of 1927 was due to firms producing too few goods. Another reason was that too few people were speculating on the stock market. Shares lost all value and the stock market finally crashed in August. There was a rush to buy shares. The value of the shares went up.

3. Explain in no more than two sentences what you know about the following:
   - Hoovervilles • Bonus Marchers
   - Rugged individualism • The phrase 'In Hoover we trusted, now we are busted.'

4. 'President Hoover did nothing to help Americans in the Depression.'
   Write a paragraph disagreeing with this statement.

5. What were the following?
   - Hobos • The dust bowl • 'Okies' • POUR

6. 'The Depression affected children more severely than any other group of people in the USA.'
   Write a paragraph disagreeing with this statement.

Key Topic 4: Roosevelt and the New Deal

1. Give five reasons why Roosevelt won the election and Hoover lost it. Place the reasons in order of importance.

2. Copy and complete the table below. In each column, show which Alphabet Agency was designed to help a certain group.

Unemployed	The old	Farmers

3. What explanation can you give for the following contradictory statements?
   - Roosevelt was a Democrat and yet some Democrats opposed the New Deal.
   - Roosevelt was accused of doing too much, and of doing too little with his New Deal.

4. Draw four concentric circles. Place the following opponents of the New Deal in rank order, beginning with the most serious in the middle and placing the least serious on the outside. Explain your first and last choices.

   - Republicans
   - Supreme Court
   - Huey Long
   - Father Coughlin

5. Group the following statements as either successes or failures of the New Deal.
   (a) It gave people confidence.
   (b) It stabilised the US banking system.
   (c) There were still fourteen million out of work in 1937.
   (d) It encouraged people to 'sponge' from the state.
   (e) Only 8000 women were employed by the CCC.
   (f) Unemployment fell from 24.9 million in 1933 to 14.3 million in 1937.
   (g) It greatly extended the role of central government.
   (h) Eleanor Roosevelt campaigned for women's rights.
   (i) It strengthened the position of trade unions.
   (j) Many New Deal agencies discriminated against black people.

6. Which statement best sums up the New Deal? Explain your choice.
   (a) The New Deal solved the immediate problems but not long-term unemployment.
   (b) The New Deal was successful in solving the problems of the Depression.
   (c) The New Deal was a total failure.

Glossary

Alphabet Agencies The bodies set up in the New Deal to tackle the problems of the Depression. They were known by their alphabetical acronyms – the Civilian Conservation Corps, for example, was the CCC.

Anarchism Belief in removing all forms of government.

Anti-Saloon League An organisation founded in 1895 which campaigned for Prohibition.

Attorney general Chief legal officer of the US government.

'Back to normalcy' Warren Harding's slogan promising a return to the more carefree days of 1917, before the USA entered the First World War.

Balance the budget Ensure that the government does not spend more than it raises in taxes.

Bible Belt Area of southern USA where Christian belief is strong.

Bolsheviks The communist group led by Lenin.

Bull market A time when share prices are rising.

Capitalism A system under which businesses are owned privately and people are able to make a profit.

Capitalists The owners of the means of production, such as factory bosses

Chaperone An older woman who accompanies a younger woman when she goes out.

Collective bargaining Negotiation of workers, represented by union leaders, with employers.

Communist A believer in the theory that society should be classless, private property abolished, and land and businesses owned collectively. Following the Communist Revolution in Russia in 1917, there had been a growing fear that communism might spread to the USA and destroy the system of government.

Congress The US equivalent of parliament. Congress is split into two parts, the Senate and the House of Representatives.

Conservative Democrats Democrats who did not want much change.

Constitution The rules under which a country is governed.

Consumer goods Manufactured goods that satisfy personal needs – vacuum cleaners, for example.

Consumerism An increase in the production of consumer goods on the grounds that high spending is the basis of a sound economy.

Credit Money available for borrowing.

Creditor One to whom a financial debt is owed.

Democratic Party One of the two main US political parties. Broadly speaking, the party is likely to agree with federal government intervention and to favour measures to improve health, welfare and education.

Depression A period of extended and severe decline in a nation's economy, marked by low production and high unemployment.

Discriminate Treat individuals unfairly because of their gender, race or religious beliefs.

Federal government The central government of the USA, based in Washington, DC.

Fireside chat One of Roosevelt's speeches to the nation. It was assumed people sat by the fire as they listened to him. The image was one of a cosy friendly chat.

Flapper A young woman who flouted norms of dress and behaviour.

General strike A strike of workers in most if not all trades.

Ghetto A city neighbourhood inhabited by a minority who live there because of social and economic pressure.

Governor The elected head of a state within the USA.

Gross National Product Total value of all goods and services in a country.

Hobo An unemployed wanderer seeking a job.

Import duties Taxes placed on goods brought from foreign countries

Industrialist Someone who owns and/or runs an industry or factory.

Infrastructure The key services upon which an economy depends, such as roads, railways, water supplies, electricity.

Isolationism A policy of deliberately staying out of world affairs. The USA was isolationist between the two world wars.

Laissez-faire A policy of non-interference by the government in industry and society.

Liberals Those who were prepared to introduce reforms in order to overcome economic problems.

Lynch To hang a person without trial.

Mass production Manufacture of goods on a large scale.

Mechanisation The use of machines.

Migrate To move from one place to another.

Minimum wage The lowest wage per hour that someone can be paid.

Negro A word used historically for a black person.

New Deal The name given to the policies introduced by President Roosevelt in the 1930s to solve the problems created by the Depression.

Patriotism Devotion to one's country and concern for its defence.

Quaker Name given to the Society of Friends, a religious group devoted to principles of peace and plainness of speech and dress.

Recession A period of declining productivity and reduced economic activity.

Relief agency Body set up to help those suffering as a result of the Depression.

Republican Party One of the two main US political parties. Broadly speaking, the party's main aims are to keep taxes low, limit the powers of the federal government and follow policies which favour business and encourage people to be self-sufficient.

Rugged individualism The American ideal that individuals are responsible for their own lives without help from anyone else; they stand or fall by their own efforts.

Segregation The separation of people on the basis of race or religion. This could include separate housing, education, health treatment and access to public buildings.

Senate The upper house of the US Congress. Each state is represented by two senators.

Sharecroppers Farm workers who did not own their land; they were given a share of the crops instead of a wage.

Socialism A system under which the government (rather than private bodies) controls the means of production.

State legislature The lawmaking body within a state.

Stock market The place where stocks and shares are bought and sold on a daily basis.

Stocks and shares Certificates of ownership in a company.

Supreme Court The highest federal court in the USA. It consists of nine judges, chosen by the president, who make sure that the president and Congress obey the rules of the Constitution.

Tariff An import duty; a tax on foreign goods coming into a country.

Temperance Movement An organisation which sought to outlaw the sale of alcoholic beverages.

Thrifty Cautious in the management of money.

Trade union An association of workers formed to improve working and living conditions.

Unconstitutional Breaking the rules of a constitution.

Veto The right to block a piece of legislation with a single vote against.

Voluntarism Relying on individuals to help out freely rather than the state interfering and imposing solutions.

Wall Street The location in New York of the USA's stock market and the headquarters of most of the nation's major financial institutions.

WASP White Anglo-Saxon Protestant

Welfare Financial assistance given by the state to individuals or families in the form of income support, for example.

White supremacy The theory that white people are naturally superior to people of other races.

Women's movement A united effort to improve the social and political position of women.

Index